My First Time
W

Advertising's
Top Women Creatives
Talk about Their First
Commercial, Ad, Or Site
And What They Learned From it

And That All You've Heard
About The Crazy World Of Advertising
Doesn't Even Come Close

Paperback ISBN 978-1-78092-299-7
ePub ISBN 978-1-78092-300-0
PDF ISBN 978-1-78092-301-7

Published in the UK by MX Publishing
335 Princess Park Manor, Royal Drive, London, N11 3GX
www.mxpublishing.com

Cover design by
www.staunch.com

This is for
Gargamel

Foreword

It's been said of Ginger Rogers:

"She did everything Fred did.
Backwards. And in high heels."

Table of Contents

Introduction

In the original *My First Time*, my introduction began like this:

"Nobody starts at the top. Nobody.

While some may be born with a silver spoon, no one is born with a Gold Pencil. Or a Gold Lion."

For the top creative ad women in the world, starting at the bottom looked good.

When I was a kid, there was a song, "It's A Woman's World". I was so little I believed it.

Don't believe it.

It seemed that the girls in my public school were always smarter than the boys. Valerie Singer, Anita Siegel, Cheryl Kurtzer. Brains. The boys were a bunch of drooling, troglodytic pinheads. I looked at the girls with awe and sadly accepted the proper order of things; which was that the girls were smarter than the boys.

The girls always won more gold stars. Got more commendations. Were class monitors more than boys. The boys were used for heavy lifting. Carry the flag during assembly. Fetch, move and set up the movie projector. Help the teacher carry the heavy books. We were a group of non-union laborers. And minors, no less. Weren't there laws against that?

Then I grew up. So did the girls. But the men were running things. Not the women.

Huh?

How the hell did things change so much? When did testosterone eclipse estrogen?

Oh, I know this all happened way before I got out of public school; probably about the time the first caveman clubbed the first cavewoman over the head. But I've never been able to shake the idea that women are smarter. Except when they marry *us*. As my far-superior-to-me-in-every-which-way wife says: "Everyone is entitled to one mistake."

When I did the original *My First Time*, as I looked through my files, I began to notice a disturbing numeric statistic among top world creatives; although I bet it's consistent in every other endeavor (except child bearing):

Top Men Creatives: Skillions
Top Women Creatives: Itsy-bitsy

This upset me on a number of levels. My mother was a woman. My wife is a woman. My daugther-in-law is a woman. And though none of them are, or were, advertising creatives, (though my daughter-in-law is an incredible planner), I just didn't get it.

I get it, but I just don't get it. I thought that we in advertising, an art, were better than that.

The ad and design schools are filled with women today; so perhaps a few decades down the pike, women will be clubbing men over the head (metaphorically speaking only).

So here, we're celebrating some of the most senior, incredibly talented, advertising women creatives in the world. Some of the stories you'll read are hilarious; some are very touching; and some are simply outrageous. You may even say: "Hey, that happened to me!" And that's the whole point. You're not the only one to go through what some of these women went through. And lived and thrived. And are telling their tales.

You'll read a story of a woman who grew up in the Amazon jungle and another who braved the winters of Finland. You'll read about spider tattoos on the tummy and hit-on-you-babe spiders of a two-legged variety.

You'll even read two of the stories in English, but also in the contributors' native languages of Spanish and Swedish, too. One from Monica Moro, the other from Anna Qvennerstedt. Can you guess which is which?

Now, who am I and how did I come to arrange this creative conclave?

I'm Phil Growick, Managing Director of the Howard-Sloan-Koller Group. In a gentle colloquialism, I'm a headhunter for top world advertising talent. Top talent who are also really top people. And I'm

8

doing it at the best executive search firm in the world (okay, so I'm a bit prejudiced here, but it's true).

In asking my friends and colleagues to write their stories for MFTW, I discovered that the women here have a not-so-secret sorority to help each other along. What a concept. Let me elaborate:

Mimi Cook, when she saw the women who were contributors, wrote to me:

"Let me know your deadline and I'll join my sisters."

It struck me as so matter-of-fact, so offhand, so natural yet so philosophically encompassing, that I just kept re-reading it.

It's one of the most generous things I've heard in advertising. But then again, other contributors sent me suggestions of top colleagues to be included and they were extremely generous in their time and thoughts, as well.

I also discovered from the stories that the term: "Who the f**k are *you*?" seems to be universal.

I'm not taking anything away from the top men creatives, at all here. But I just want to let the women shine alone in this volume. They certainly deserve it.

From everything I've heard, read and experienced myself, they've had more of an uphill battle than we Y chromosomers.

But as the old adage goes, X marks the spot.

It does here, at least.

A Guide To Creative Title Acronyms

(This is for anyone reading who may be a civilian – not in the ad industry)

Some people insist that advertising has as many acronyms for their creative people as the Pentagon does for their most oblique designations. And they would be correct. But the Pentagon has a better precision ratio.

So to help you fathom any acronym that may creep into the stories you're about to read, here are some basic explanations, starting from the top:

CCO: Chief Creative Officer

At larger agencies, this is the top position in the advertising infirmament. The CCO is treated like a god, and is appreciative of being remembered during Christmas and/or Yom Kippur.

The CCO is held responsible for the entire creative output of the agency, is held hostage by every client, and, in basic truth, just wants to be held.

ECD: Executive Creative Director

In some agencies, the top creative position. And as the title states, is the one who executes the creative directors.

GCD: Group Creative Director

This person is responsible for a group of accounts and a group of creative teams who are responsible for the creative product for those accounts. However, these teams will only group
around their GCD with of the Ides of March in mind.

CD: Creative Director

At smaller agencies, this is the top creative person, in charge of all accounts and all creatives.

At larger shops, the CD manages an account or two, a team or two, and is the first to group around the GCD on the Ides of March. Seeing a pattern here?

ACD: Associate Creative Director
The only people who will associate with the creative director.

CW: Copywriter
This is one half of a creative team; the one who flunked English, was thrown out of journalism school, and who's grasp of basic punctuation makes what they've written look like Sanskrit on a bad day.

AD: Art Director
The other half of a creative team; the one who sits and draws pretty pictures all day while growing a moustache like Salvador Dali, a beard like Leonardo DaVinci, and acts like Duchamps' "Nude Descending A Staircase".

So there you have it, the basic explanations of who does what. And who does what to whom.

And now,
the totally true stories…

Rosie Arnold

Deputy Executive Creative Director of BBH, London
President, D&AD

Rosie started moonlighting at a tiny creative hot shop called Bartle Bogle Hegarty in 1983 while studying at Central St Martins. She has been there ever since. Always motivated by the opportunity to do mould breaking creative work amongst like-minded people, she has had no reason to move.

She spent the formative years of her career working closely with John Hegarty, learning the trade. In her time to date she has been responsible for some of the Agency's most iconic work from Pretty Polly and Levi's in the 80s; The Independent, TAG, Robinsons and Omo. She lead Axe (Lynx) for 14 years and more recently is behind the latest phenomenon that is Yeo Valley.

Her work has amassed many awards including six Cannes Gold, six D&AD pencils and three Campaign Golds.

My First Time
By Rosie Arnold

Having managed to land myself a job in a tiny creative hot shop called Bartle Bogle Hegarty, the next thing I had to do was come up with a fantastic campaign that would make John Hegarty proud of me and send my career into giddying heights and win me a much coveted D&AD yellow pencil.

Clasping my 6 layouts for a Pretty Polly stocking print campaign - dreams of walking up to podiums in my mind - I entered the meeting room to present my treasured idea.

The client who I have conveniently forgotten, systematically destroyed those dreams. He found it difficult to imagine why Venice was remotely glamorous as a location, why weren't we showing acres of leg, and what were we doing aiming the campaign at women?

Lesson No. 1 - A wise head keepeth a still tongue
        The client also couldn't quite understand that I was an art director and not a secretary or a bit of fluff laid on for his entertainment.

Lesson No. 2 - There are not many women in the creative side of the business and it is not a good idea to slap a client
        Somehow despite the inauspicious start, we sold the work and I found myself in heaven choosing a photographer - anyone I liked!
I asked my group head Graham Watson for his recommendations, poured over magazines, went to galleries, etc. until I had quite a list. We called all the portfolios in and so I wouldn't be influenced by a famous name I removed all the names form the portfolios before going through them.

Lesson No. 3 - Don't EVER do this again –

Unless you want to spend dizzying amounts of time trying to match up the work with the name.

I chose the one I liked best and it turned out to be the statuesque and extremely famous Terence Donovan.

Lesson No. 4 - There's a reason people become famous
They really are better than other people and that's why they become famous.

My joy and disbelief that this was a real job, and that it was mine, knew no bounds.
I was going to Venice with Terence Donovan to shoot a print campaign, and the stylist was a certain Liz Tilberis, the then-editor of British Vogue. Gulp.

Lesson No. 5 - This is the best job in the world
And however junior you are you get incredible opportunities.

Arriving in Venice and talking to our model I discovered that she and I were the same age but she was being paid more for 3 days work than I was getting for 2 years.

Lesson No. 6 - Maybe it isn't the best job in the world

It was November and the streets were flooded, no not the canals, the streets. Everything was closing up and romantic though it undoubtedly was, we couldn't get a permit. Terence had an idea. He sent the model, Liz, and the make-up artist into the Ca D'Oro on the Grand Canal.

The model wore her gorgeous evening gown and patterned tights disguised under a cloak with instructions to slip through security and out on to the balcony - we would be waiting on the opposite side, camera at the ready.

Lesson No. 7 - You need to be brave determined and inventive to get the perfect shot

He dressed me up and I posed on the opposite side of the canal and amazingly the model slipped through security and appeared on the balcony, Terence, dressed in full army camouflage (quite why in the middle of Venice I will never know), swung the camera round and photographed our model. I was 22 (just) and found the whole experience dazzling.

The shot was perfect.

Triumphantly we returned home and although the campaign was only nominated for a pencil, just getting in the book was a thrill for me and my then partner, Kiki Kendrick.

However there was an unexpected side to the shoot that both Kiki and I had to deal with and (watch out girls) it seemed to happen a lot throughout my career: unwelcome attention from guys who believe that just because you're out of the country you're fair game. It wasn't really a problem, because I was very clear that was not a path I was going to follow.

I look back now and laugh at some of the more outrageous things that were said to me, like: "I could pull you on like a wet wellington."!! UGH!. But at the time it could be intimidating. I hope that these days everyone has moved on. But be prepared.

Last Lesson- You can be bubbly, enthusiastic, care about your appearance but make sure you have a good range of charming rebuttals up your sleeves.

I realise just how lucky I was to have landed my first job at a place like BBH. I'm still here and each new project still has the thrill of my first time.

Last lesson - Do things because they interest or excite you, and interesting and exciting things will happen to you.

Sarah Barclay
Executive Creative Director
JWT, New York

Originally from London, Sarah moved to Australia when she was 6 years old. She completed a degree in Visual Communication at Art College in Sydney and went on to receive top student honors at AWARD School. At The Campaign Palace Melbourne she won best TV commercial in 25 years in Australia for Antz Pantz. In 1999 she and her partner were ranked number 10 in Boards Award's Top Creative Teams in the world.

Sarah moved to BBDO New York in 2000; then in 2003 joined Saatchi & Saatchi as Global Creative Director on P&G brands.

She is now an Executive Creative Director at JWT New York working on Energizer, Unilever and Nestle.

Over the years she has helped create award-winning campaigns on myriad brands ranging from tampons and razors to milk, laundry and airlines. She has also served on many international award show juries including Cannes and D&AD.

My First Time
By Sarah Barclay

Ten lessons from ten firsts.

1. Invent.

My writer and I were at a small agency in Sydney working on an uninteresting project. AIDS had just started to get media attention and condom use was being encouraged so we decided to write a print campaign promoting condoms. We had no idea what we would do with it. A journalist for a national magazine heard about the project and contacted us. We had our first campaign. The magazine ended up running 5 single page ads, they got loads of publicity and the CD of one of the most creative shops in Australia offered us jobs.

2. Try something that might not work.

My first TV ad was for a brand of women's shoes called Candy. Our idea involved a girl pulling a stiletto out of her mouth. This was before CG had really been embraced by the ad industry so it had to all be done in camera. We were filming in a men's toilet block in a park using a collapsible shoe and had no idea if we could pull it off (or out). We got it on the 29th take, dribble and all.

3. Craft, craft, craft.

I couldn't find a typeface I wanted for my first headline driven print ad. It had bastard in the headline and I wanted the art direction to be as just as ballsy. I manipulated and destroyed a face using a photocopier, a scalpel and a pencil. It took me days.

4. Find a mentor.

I was lucky enough to have worked for the best boss in the world at The Campaign Palace Melbourne. He was able to spot a great idea from a hundred scribbles on the floor. My writer and I had work plastered everywhere in our office and Scott walked in on his way to lunch and gazed around the room before nodding at a sheet of paper involving ants, a woman's crotch and an anteater. It went on to win our first ever gold.

5. Say no to money.

Take the low paying job at a good agency. Money, and maybe fame, will follow. My first job paid $14,000.

6. Be a planner.

My partner and I were pitching for a milk account at Clemenger BBDO in Melbourne. We loved the insight that children were jokingly attributed to the local milko if they didn't look like their dad. We knew this was an interesting truth about milk that no other drink could own and came up with a campaign based around the legendary status of milkmen. We won the pitch with the idea, the ads went to air unchanged and they won awards. That was definitely a great first.

7. Study.

I know an art director who can recall nearly every award-winning idea for decades. Not only is it important to know what's been done, you will be constantly inspired. My first few years were spent poring over award annuals, reels and magazines searching out the best ideas from all over the world. Now the world is at your fingertips so there's no excuse not to know that great VW Polo ad with the singing dog.

8. Be a presenter.

I remember my first client presentation in New York. I was working with my partner from Yorkshire who has quite a strong northern English accent. No one could tell our accents apart, even though we sounded completely different. They called us The Australians. They always asked if the girl one could present because no one could understand the boy one. Having an accent is a definite plus. Or do a presentation course.

9. You oughta be congratulated.

This was one of the reasons I was inspired to get into advertising. I was at art college and there was a TV ad at the time that congratulated mums for buying a particular brand of margarine. It made my skin crawl. I was inspired to do an ad campaign for my final year project and won an internship at my first agency straight from college. It's important to stay true to what you believe, especially in an industry that is still pretty much a boy's club.

10. Jump.

There's nothing like stepping out of your comfort zone. My first job out of Australia was like starting a whole other life. My work partner and I won a trip to New York for some Yellow Pages posters we'd done and were offered a job in New York in the first week we were there. Living and working here for the last 11 years has been a bloody fabulous experience.

I also learnt that you really just have to get in there and have a go. Will Rogers was right. There are three kinds of men. The ones that learnt by readin'. The few who learnt by observation. The rest of them have to pee on the electric fence for themselves.

Lisa Bennett

Chief Creative Officer
North American Creative Chair
DDB, San Francisco

Lisa began her career at Leo Burnett after graduating from The University of Texas in Austin. She became a Creative Director at age 27 and in 2000 Advertising Age named Lisa one of "21 to Watch in the 21st Century". She went on to lead the creative charge on iconic brands such as McDonald's, Disney, Coca Cola, Delta Airlines and Heinz Ketchup.

In 2003, Lisa joined DDB as Managing Partner & Chief Creative Officer of the San Francisco office. Over the years, she has attracted world-class talent and brought a new energy and recognition to the agency's creative product. Within two years of her arrival, DDB SF won their first Cannes Lion and a few years later received four Cannes Lions across four different categories. Under Lisa's leadership, the team has created award-winning campaigns for Glad, Brita, Kingsford and attracted new clients to the agency such as Intel, ConAgra, ESPN International, and Benefit Cosmetics.

This past year, Lisa added North American Creative Chair to her responsibilities. In Her new role, she leads the DDB North American Creative Council and sits on the Global Creative Council as the North American representative. Lisa has served on The Cannes Lions Film jury and Executive juries for One Show, CLIO Awards, Communication Arts and New York Festivals.

My First Time
By Lisa Bennett

The first thing I ever produced was a four-line poem published on Valentine's Day by The Austin American Statesman. I was 7. From that day on I knew I wanted to be a writer when I grew up. Or an artist. Or a musician. Or David Cassidy's wife. I kept a journal, learned to paint, play piano and clarinet, and never missed an episode of The Partridge Family.

I was accepted into The University of Texas on a music scholarship, but changed majors after one semester. I missed writing and drawing. I also missed a lot of 8am Clarinet section rehearsals. (Wednesday night sorority mixers + Thursday morning music rehearsals = C+). Fortunately, I found a class in the course curriculum called *Creative Advertising 101* that combined the other two things I loved and knew I had found my calling.

I spent the next three years writing, drawing and dating my future husband (who is much cuter and much taller than David Cassidy). At the end of the fall semester of my senior year, I was showing my portfolio to a recruiter from Leo Burnett. "Are you a writer or an art director?" She asked. "What would you like me to be?" I answered.

The next semester I graduated with a BS in Advertising. Two days later I moved to Chicago, started at Burnett (as an art director), flew back to Austin, got married, went back to work and sold my first TV spot (as a writer). There were words and pictures, but that's about all I remember. And not just because I was on a honeymoon high. In those days, Burnett had a training program where the creative teams rotated to a new group every three months. I had sold my first commercial and because I had to move on, someone else produced it. So, technically, I wasn't even there for my first time.

A few weeks into the next rotation, my new partner and I sold a print campaign for Black & Decker. Once again, the shoot was "handled" by the ACD. When our three months were up we left our dreams of shooting power tools on black sweeps behind and gladly moved on to the next group. It was one of the best in the agency with talented, fun people and iconic brands like McDonald's and Hallmark.

Within a few months, I had my third first. I sold another spot. But not for one of the high-profile accounts (which is probably why the assignment was given to a junior team). It was a pool out for the Heinz Gravy campaign. And this time, nothing was going to stop me from going on that production. As a "seasoned" art director with a good 7 ½ months of experience under my belt, I knew enough to know that I needed to be on that shoot. I had to bring my idea to life. I had to cast funny people and select average looking wardrobe. I had to make sure the pours and stirs and bites and smiles were perfect. I had to choose the gravy boat, damnit! But first, I would have to do some serious convincing that a completely green 22 year-old should be attending the most important jarred condiment shoot in history.

Turned out, not that much convincing was needed. There were no other ACD's in this group that wanted to handle my gravy shoot. Plus, my boss was a big believer in allowing juniors to jump right into production. Not to call the shots, but to help realize the ideas that came out of their heads. And to learn. Because who knew that to get the perfect pour shot, one had to have the perfect roast beef underneath it. And to get the perfect roast beef, about 50 pounds of it has to be cooked on the set (causing it to reek for two days and your hair to reek for another three). And who knew that the "less cool" account that nobody wanted to work on would be the one that finally earns you recognition and helps the agency win more business from that client.

My first time was far from glamorous, but I did learn a lot from the experience. I learned to be patient. To relentlessly pursue what I believe in. That you can build a very successful career around offering to take on the projects nobody else wants to. And I learned to treat every time as if it were my first.

Pip Bishop
Creative Partner
RKCR/Y&R

Pip first passed herself off as a copywriter at Cogent, London, in 1984. Together with her long-suffering art director, Chris, she created award-winning work for Milton Keynes, Epson Printers and Cuprinol.

In 1991, she moved to Hoare Wilkins, where she created a hard-hitting campaign to save Charing Cross Hospital and a rather more contentious one for Death Cigarettes .

She joined TBWA in 1992, where she fed her addiction for kitsch cop shows by producing the Professionals and Sweeney spoofs for the Nissan Almera, and got her own back on mankind by creating the Nissan Micra "Ask before You borrow it" campaign.

With several challenging merges under her belt, and longing for the intimacy of a smaller agency, she arrived at Rainey Kelly Campbell Roalfe in 1999 (6 months before they merged with Y&R!). Early highlights included the Rik

Mayall campaign for Virgin Trains, Thorntons' Chocolate Heaven and the love it/hate it "fat bird running up a hill" slot for Marks & Spencer.

She was promoted to Creative Director in 2000 and has been there ever sinceHer highlights have included the multi-awarded Virgin Atlantic 'Still Red Hot' and 'It' campaigns and the last nine star-spangled Christmas spots for M & S. She is currently working on number ten...

My First Time
By Pip Bishop

First Agency: A smallish UK independent a couple of D&ADs short of a creative hot-shop (name withheld to protect the guilty).

First Salary: £5,000 per annum

First Print ad: ICI Weedkiller

First Poster: Milton Keynes 6 sheet

First TV Commercial: Budgen Supermarkets Offer ad

First bit of career advice: "No girl creative has ever lasted more than 6 months here unless they sleep with the boss".

It was week one in my first agency. I looked round. There was only one other girl in a department of 20. She'd been there for 5 years. Work it out.

I was horrified, but more than that, angry. I'd got this job against all odds after a serious motorbike accident in the middle of my degree course had put me in hospital for months. Did my future career really just hang by my knicker elastic?

I took a deep breath, drew on my vast resources of stroppy stubborn Northern-ness, and decided to keep my knickers on.

I 'lasted' there for 8 years.

In the mid to late 80s, the female creative was very rare indeed. In London, you could count most of us on two hands. The ones that survived had thick skins, worked hard and had great senses of humour. And they usually trod that fine line between feminine and fearless.

Over the years, the occasions when I've thought that being a woman might have got in the way of great work have been few and far between. My long-term partner Chris is male, so I never got lumbered with that 'girl team' tag (and the ensuing san-pro briefs), but mainly because I never expected to be treated any differently from anyone else. I thank hard work for my successes and blame lack of talent or application for my failures.

When I worked at TBWA in the 90s I was part of Trevor Beattie's incredibly bawdy, incredibly quick-witted and very male department. I got wind of the fact that the boys' nickname for me was 'The Stone'. After lengthy investigation, I discovered that it stood for 'The stone in the shoe of the creative department'. I pretended to be slightly hurt, but to be honest, I thought it was absolutely hilarious.

I'll leave you with a few bits of career advice of my own:

If you act like a minority, you'll be treated like one.

Make sure you're as good at working on cars as cosmetics.

Don't go running to HR every time you hear something vaguely offensive.

Don't let anyone tell you that you can't do something.

And finally… keep your knickers on.

Jeanie Caggiano
EVP/Executive Creative Director/Writer
Leo Burnett, Chicago

Unlike every other creative in advertising, Jeanie Caggiano is still in her first job.

One humid day in August, 1983, she rode the El train to Leo Burnett for the first time.

Ever since, she's told stories for Leo's flagship clients: Allstate, Hallmark, Kellogg's, McDonald's, Philip Morris and Procter & Gamble. As well as lesser-known luminaries like Prozac and Exclusive Resorts. Along the way, she picked up all of the requisite awards except for a Cannes Grand Prix. Hey—there's still time.

The moment that turned Jeanie from writer to change agent came in 2003, when Leo Burnett was about to be fired by Allstate. She came up with the "Our Stand" campaign featuring actor Dennis Haysbert. Over the next 8 years, it won many awards including a Silver Lion and double-digit Effies, including a gold for Sustained Success.

For one Allstate spot, Jeanie shot a car off the 17th floor of the iconic Marina Towers building into the Chicago River. After the shoot, an OOH installation hung a car halfway off the same floor. It wasn't just noticed by award juries; it also got a bunch of concerned citizens to call 911.

Seven years later, at another crisis moment (new Allstate CMO), Jeanie was behind the gleefully destructive Mayhem. She knew he was a success when, just three months after launch, more than one trick-or-treater came to her door dressed in a suit, wearing a pink headband and carrying pink barbells.

In 2012, after 11 years on Allstate, Jeanie realized she was bored. So she decided to become a change agent on other brands looking for a creative turnaround. She currently heads up Hallmark Cards and WhiteWave Foods (Silk, International Delight Coffee Creamer and Horizon Organic Milk).

A published poet, Jeanie is married with two kids in grade school. She also takes ballet religiously, twice a week, in whatever city she happens to find herself. It's been mandatory ever since she gained ten pounds her first winter at Leo Burnett. Why? Eating too many Keebler cookies.

My First Time
By Jeanie Caggiano

Each time is my first time.

Each time I stare at a blank piece of paper.

Or now, more often, at the hopeful faces of the creatives who bring me pieces of paper that were once blank.

Every creative thinks their Creative Director is just dying to kill their idea, slap it down, piss on it.

Not true.

Internally, we're going, "Please have something good. Please have something I haven't seen before. Please have something that changes my mind, stirs my heart, or makes me laugh out loud."

And it's only when we don't see it that we have to say, "No. Try again." But if there's one thing I've learned, it's that writing something is better than writing nothing. Things all start from something.

I was in my senior year at Northwestern. On a whim, I took an advertising class. It was like the heavens opened up and a light shone down on me and a voice said, "This, stupid! *This* is what you were born to do!"

It was the spring, and companies were interviewing on campus. I saw Leo Burnett was there, and I signed up. A nice man named Ashton Lee interviewed me. I guess we hit it off okay, because he invited me downtown for a full day of interviews. What I didn't understand at the time was that the job he was recruiting for was account executive.

The Leo Burnett tradition was that on the night before your interview, a junior account exec would take you out to dinner and prep you for the interview. I rode down on the El, and met a nice young woman named Kathy somebody at a restaurant called Toulouse.

This was 1982. Men ruled the world of business, and this was a businessman's restaurant. We were the only two women in the place. So guys started sending over drinks. At one point, we each had 12 glasses of varying colors of wine in front of us. I guess the guys were hoping we'd get drunk and stumble out of the restaurant so they could spirit us away. The problem was, I couldn't drink a drop. Because I'd caught the flu. So in between courses, I'd excuse myself to go to the bathroom and throw up. I remember I had Chicken Kiev because I tasted it a lot. I don't remember the El ride home. Apparently, I made it. Because I showed up at Burnett bright and early the next day. In a suit with shoulder pads.

I had 8 interviews. And every one was memorable, because of what I'd written on my blank page. In those days, Leo Burnett asked every aspiring account person for a 200-word writing sample. The subject: anything. I suppose some smarties wrote 200 words on "The Penetration of 2-Ply Toilet Paper in DMAs in the Southern United States." Not me. The title of my writing sample was "Why I am A Penguin".

Every single interviewer said, "Wow—this is really well written. Don't you want to be a creative?" To the first interviewer, I said, "Why? Don't you guys write the ads?" After that, I kept my mouth shut.

The last interviewer was a guy named Mike Hall. He was 6'2", a former Marine, served in Vietnam. And the only African-American account guy Burnett had. He looked at me and spit out, "Are you touuuuuugh, girl? In this business, you gotta be touuuuuugh!"

"I'm tough," I squeaked.

The rejection letter arrived two days later.

34

But, being persistent (good trait in this business), and tough (though I didn't know it then), I called Ashton Lee and said, "I know you guys nuked me, but I really want to be in advertising. What should I do?" He told me to go to grad school.

So I did - an account exec program at Northwestern. But there were 3 or 4 poor souls every year who wanted to be creatives instead, and ended up in the wrong place because they didn't know any better. An alum who'd been in the same pickle and was now a writer at Burnett came down in the spring, showed us his spec book and told us we had to put one together if we wanted to be creatives.

I put my book together, graduated from NU, rode down on the El to Leo Burnett again, and was hired by Huntley Baldwin to work on the Keebler Elves and Ronald McDonald. Since then, I've done work for Hallmark, McDonald's, Prozac, Disney, and most recently, Allstate; where we've created many things—including a little bit of Mayhem.

If there's a lesson to be learned from any of this, I guess it's "Don't just stare at the page. Write something." Oh, and keep a copy. Nearly three decades later, I have no idea why I was a penguin.

Mimi Cook
Former Brand Strategy Director
Mekanism

Mimi grew up in a little town called Modesto, California -- and she is fairly certain because at birth, she went home from the hospital in the wrong station wagon. Her love of words and language lead her to attend the University of California, Berkeley, where she studied comparative literature and Latin.

Her career in advertising began at Chiat/Day, San Francisco. From there, she went on to work at a few other amazing shops (F.C.B., Hal Riney & Partners, Goodby, Silverstein & Partners) on some amazing brands (Saturn, Banana Republic, Levi's, Michelob).

Mimi has also worked as a creative director at Apple, Inc. on the launch of two of the company's most lauded products, iPhone and iPad. Her love of branding and social media then lead her to become a Brand Strategy Director at Mekanism.

Along the way, she's been recognized by Cannes, Communication Arts, the Clios, D&AD, and The One Show. Ad Age also honored her as a

"Woman to Watch" and featured her work for Levi's as one of the 50 Best TV Commercials in 50 Years of Advertising. Only a handful of people know that Mimi is also the reigning "Queen of Analogies," likes to run the hills of Berkeley with her chihuahua Emmett, and has two daughters, who she was sure that up until this moment would get published before she did.

My First Time
By Mimi Cook

Growing up, I was clueless about what I wanted to be in life. Even when I took a high school class promisingly called "Careers," my worst fears were confirmed. A computer print-out stated I was 100% perfect for a "Real Estate Agent" or "Singer/Performer." Having failed the audition for 4th grade chorus, I was pretty sure that only left "Real Estate Agent" -- and I was pretty sure that wasn't going to work.

The only career I saw as a kid that looked remotely interesting to me was on old reruns of The Dick Van Dyke Show. In fact, you could say the character of Rose Marie was my first true mentor. Here's why: in every single episode, she spitballed with a team of fast talking comedy writers -- all men -- and held her own. Plus she rocked a pencil skirt and pumps like nobody's business.

It wouldn't be until after I graduated from college and registered with a job placement agency that I finally saw what the world had to offer. They sent me on an interview with a company I'd never heard of, Chiat/Day. That I'd be in the media department making $14,000 a year seemed like something I couldn't ignore, given the opportunity ahead of me. I was the happiest media department assistant on the face of the earth. I finally had a path -- and I was around people who probably couldn't be in any other kind of career either.

During that first year though, I kept looking over the fence at the Creative Department. They never mentioned something like that in Careers class. But that's where I wanted to be. So in my spare time, I began volunteering for creative assignments. And sometimes, I wouldn't even ask. I would just go ahead and do the work on my own and show up with it.

Like the time that we had a car account and the client needed names for the new minivan they were launching.

I spent several nights coming up multiple pages of names, most of them awful but perfect for an era that brought us shoulder pads. A few days before the big brain storming session, I found the executive creative director after hours and handed him my ideas. Poor Ross. He didn't have a clue who I was. If you can picture Gepetto awkwardly chuckling and politely thanking you, that's what I saw.

But that Friday, the moment I'd waited for came.

Chiat/Day hosted a naming session with the client in our luxurious main conference room. It went on for hours. In fact, it even went on after hours. And I stayed late right along with them at my little media assistant desk, just, you know, *in case*.

And then, my phone rang.
"Mimi! This is Ross...."
Oh. My. God.
"Yes, Ross?!"
"We're all sitting in here in the main conference room and you know what?"
"Yes?!"
"Everyone's gone home and...we are completely out of coffee."
"...."
"Would you mind making us a fresh pot and bringing it in here?"

So, yes, I made the pot of coffee. And as I pushed the thermos through the small, discreet opening between the kitchen and the conference room, it didn't go unnoticed by me that all the other side would ever see of me was just a set of hands.

My big break came a few months later when the copy typist went on maternity leave. I was offered her position, which is kind of a miracle since I'm neither a fast typist nor a good speller.

Though the job may sound like drudgery, for someone who'd never been to ad school, it was perfect. Essentially, being a typist gave me a chance to go to school on the work of super talented writers -- and at the same time, scope out all the assignments they didn't want to touch. My bottom feeding approach definitely paid off since within a month I landed an assignment that was epically unappealing: radio for Kaufman and Broad Homes.

My story at this point is basically a happy one. I wrote a :60 script, that at first was probably more like two minutes. After showing it around to any writer who'd listen -- and finally grasping the importance of a stop watch -- I refined it and presented it, the creative director approved it, the client signed off on it, and within a few weeks, I was in production on my very first commercial. (Forgive me for bragging, but I even took home a gold medal for it, the prestigious California Home Builders Association Best In Broadcast Award.)

Probably the biggest gift of all was the generosity of the writers who worked at Chiat/Day at the time. I definitely initiated a lot of questions and continually asked for input, but what was so striking was how willing they were to share what they knew.

For every new creative out there, I hope that's still true.

Vida Cornelious
Chief Creative Officer
GlobalHue

"If you're not part of the solution, you're part of the problem."
These strong words set forth by political activist Eldridge Cleaver are ones Vida Cornelious not only believes, but also has used as a guiding principle throughout her career in advertising. As a Creative Director, it is this philosophy that has allowed her to view every creative assignment as one of great challenge and ultimately, great reward.

A former 10-year veteran of DDB Chicago and VP Creative Director, in 2009 Vida decided to filter her general market creative acumen, back to the multicultural sector. She is currently leading the creative evolution of veteran multicultural agency, GlobalHue.

Under her leadership, as Chief Creative Officer, GlobalHue has won and retains general market AOR status for the Chrysler Group's Jeep brand. The win was a controversial one as it garnered press and stirred discussion regarding the firepower of multicultural agencies and their expertise in mining insights to service a more diverse marketplace. Vida's position on the subject is clear: "I am a firm believer that great ideas are based in truth, human truths that are filtered through the cultural lense of the consumer. We live in a very ethnically influenced world and it is shortsighted of a marketer to think that ignoring a consumer's exposure to diverse backgrounds and value systems is not going to effect their choices and ultimately shift brand loyalty and spark new brand conversations. The connection between consumers and brands has changed and understanding multicultural insights is the future of building successful total market integrated campaigns."

Over her 17-year advertising creative career, Vida Cornelious has created award-winning campaigns for a variety of blue chip accounts including McDonald's, Coca-Cola, Dell Computers, Budweiser, Qwest Communications, Sears, Walmart and most recently Jeep.

Her work has been recognized at Cannes International Advertising Festival, Chicago Creative Club, London International Awards, The Effie's, Summit international Awards, The Addy's, The Tellys and The D-Show. She garnered accolades for her creativity as well as for generating marketing results, thus her creative work and career have been featured in noted media outlets; Time Magazine, Advertising Age, AdWeek, Shoot, and Diversity in Business. In 2008, she was honored as an ADCOLOR "Change Agent" award winner, one of AdAge's "40 Women to Watch in Advertising of 2009" and listed on Black Enterprise's coveted "Top Minority Executives in Advertising and Marketing."

A lover of jazz, flowers and Pinterest, she is also a formidable opponent on Words with Friends and Scramble with Friends.

My First Time
By Vida Cornelious

I will be totally honest: I would never have found my way into this business had it not been for a very generous college professor who opened my eyes to the world of advertising as a career choice. There was no flowery language, mind you; no *Mr. Holland's Opus* inspired talks between us. Nope, he was not that kind of guy.

As an art professor, his criticism was direct, curt and downright cruel at times. Little did I know, exposure to those very qualities would be my best preparation for a creative career. So when I pushed for his enlightenment on what to do with myself and my fine art degree after graduation, his point of view was true to form:

> *"Vida, you are talented enough to be a designer, sure. But why? They make no money. They are bitter and draw type. Go to grad school, study advertising and be an art director. They make lots of money and TV commercials."*

Sold.

I now had a plan that could convince my parents my education was not worthless. I would make lots of money and TV commercials. At 21, it sounded reasonable enough.

Sparing you the gory details of my grad school education, subsequent addiction to marshmallow treats, obsessive reading of Maxine Paetro's *How To Put Your Book Together and Get A Job In Advertising,* internship woes and the like, I did manage to emerge from the University of Illinois ad program with an M.S. in Advertising and a portfolio good enough to get me a few interviews and finally (*add drumroll here*) "a job."

I landed at 20 N. Michigan Avenue in Chicago, IL. It was 1994. I stood in the lobby of Burrell Communications Group on my first day reporting for work. Spanking brand new black portfolio case chock full of my best stuff, new suit (I would quickly find out wearing a suit as a creative was a no-no), fresh hairdo and $6.00 for lunch. I was on top of the world.

Well, until I met my first creative director. He would be my Obi-Wan Kenobi of kerning, my Shaman of spray mount on many of my newbie assignments. That first day, I think he disapproved of me (or maybe it was my suit?) on sight. He was a gruff little man. About 50% of his body was beard and shaggy hair. He mumbled a lot and was a stickler for misspellings. His laugh was a loud cackle typically followed by the explicative *"Muddafuccas!"*

I remember him asking to see my portfolio. I mean, he didn't hire me; Alma Hopkins, the ECD, did. I was nervous and jittery as he turned the stiff acetate pages. He was eerily quiet. No comments. No criticisms. After he got through all five campaigns (because that is what Maxine Paetro's book said I needed to get a job: five campaigns!), all I got from him was a shrug of the shoulders. Four years of college, two years of grad school and eight pounds of excess college weight — essentially my creative net worth — summed up in a shoulder shrug from a guy who looked like the fourth Bee-Gee. But he was my appointed creative director, I was his appointed junior creative and that nonverbal communication told me I was officially mediocre in his mind. Let us not forget, this was DAY ONE on the job.

Every day going forward, he gave me tough love, mentoring me in a way that made me feel like I was the "little turd" he was destined (or relegated) to polish.

I completed many print assignments that he painstakingly nit-picked: the type choices, the colors, the headline placements, you name it. Not only was nothing EVER right; all of my design choices were infinitely wrong. But as his criticisms got harsher, my designs got better and my skin got thicker. I sold a few print ads, did a few photo shoots and then one day when I expertly marked up a proof with my retouching remarks, he said the words I never thought he'd be willing to say: *"Hey, you're a good muddafuccing art director."*

Music to my ears.

This proclamation earned me the chance to compete with other teams on a TV assignment. I was finally "in the game"! Coca-Cola's Sprite brand was looking for *"a multicultural interpretation of their general market campaign Obey Your Thirst."*

They want a **what?** *(Add dramatic organ music here... dunh, dunh, dunh...!)*

I stared at that brief for hours, dumbfounded. I somehow thought the later I stayed in the office, the better my chances of having one of those famous late-night creative breakthroughs, like Angela Bauer used to have on *Who's the Boss*. No dice. Once again, my short, hairy creative director appeared in my cube offering his strange blend of emotional terrorism wrapped around genuine guidance:

"You're not gonna find the muddafuccin' answer staring at that page. The answer's gonna come from you. What makes you see it different?"

That was the best advice I ever got.

I went on to sell a campaign for the effort, so I officially consider it "MY FIRST TIME." The campaign was called "Freestyle." It was full of hip-hop celebrities and was one of Sprite's most successful efforts to bring hip hop music to the mainstream. At the time, hip hop was my life. It was my recreation, education, motivation… I knew it, understood it. This was a genre of music and a lifestyle that celebrated the artistry of one's instincts — or as we connected it to the Sprite brand, a way for our multicultural soda-drinking target to "obey their thirst."

Truthfully, urban culture was a part of me. Just like my creative director had said, I realized used what I knew to uniquely tap in to something that solved the assignment, and it worked. Needless to say, I got a lot more TV assignments put on my desk after that. My confidence grew and those creative briefing documents didn't scare me so much anymore.

Ultimately, I moved on from my beginnings at Burrell and into the general market world of DDB Chicago. I was fortunate to work for other great creative directors and clients along the way, all of whom continued to "polish" me. I did more TV; I won awards; I managed teams of my own. But I never forgot that valuable piece of advice from my Bee-Gee-lookalike first creative director and now very good friend.

As an African American, as a woman and as a creative in this business, the road was never easy. I feel like I've had 1000 "first times" over the years of my career, as there has always been someone who wanted to question my ability and expertise.

Good thing I still have that thick skin when I need it.

What I had to learn is that all of the experiences and interests that make me different and make me diverse are exactly the strengths I can draw upon to inform my unique point of view. This is what gives me the ability to see the problem differently and arrive at the solution differently as well. To this day, I value that and ask the creatives I lead, value that fact about themselves as well.

In the end, I guess we all start out as "little turds" in this business. But it's the lessons you learn and the way you use them to develop your work, style, leadership and character that give you all the polish you need to shine.

Susan Credle
Chief Creative Officer, Leo Burnett North America

Every agency says it wants "to do great creative," but for Chief Creative Officer Susan Credle, it's the reason why that matters.

"Great creative has to build helpful, meaningful brands for the long-term," she says. "That's the sum of what we at Leo Burnett do, and what I've set out to do my entire career."

It's a career that began — and we swear we're not cribbing a plotline from Mad Men — covering the phones for receptionists at BBDO New York during their bathroom breaks.

Susan soon, though, began sharing her ideas with the creative department, and "three months later, I got on a desk as an assistant. A year later I became a junior writer."

By the time she joined Leo Burnett in the fall of 2009, she had risen at

BBDO to EVP Executive Creative Director. She was known throughout the advertising industry for her reinvention and 15-year stewardship of M&M's iconic characters as well as for helping to launch Cingular Wireless and ultimately turn it into a leader brand.

These experiences, along with consistently awarded work for such clients as Pepsi, FedEx, Lowe's, Bank of America and Visa, taught her the value of breathing new life into rather than discarding brand equities while at the same time starting legacies for the next generation.

"I also learned that companies can do large-scale communications that benefit their brands and the world," she says.

Sharing these lessons with both veteran creatives and the top new talent she has attracted to Leo Burnett, Susan has spearheaded a creative renaissance at the agency. Her leadership, inspiration and in-the-trenches contributions have led to legacy-respecting yet forward-looking campaigns for Leo Burnett clients like McDonald's, Allstate, Kellogg's, P&G, Sealy and Invesco.

Susan's work on Happy Meal "Happy Tales" campaign, for example, is helping to bring together groundbreaking artists and musicians to give kids and parents quality storytelling while allowing McDonald's to return the brand to its iconic roots.

For P&G's Secret, she has overseen a "Mean Stinks" campaign that has inspired thousands of teenage girls to share their stories, advice and friendship in an effort to wipe out bullying — and given the deodorant brand meaning in their lives.

And then, of course, there's Allstate's "Mayhem," one of the most beloved and talked-about campaigns in years.

"We don't have a house style," Susan likes to say. "The work should all look unique, because each of our clients is unique."

My First Time
By Susan Fowler Credle

In 1985, I didn't know that while a one-way ticket to Newark from North Carolina was only $39, the taxi to 63rd and Park would be $50 before tip. So much for that $100 to get me started in NYC.

I didn't know that a BA in Journalism from the University of North Carolina couldn't even land you a job as a secretary (somewhere between then and now the name changed to assistant) if you were unable to type 60 wpm flawlessly. A BA in typing or bartending would have been a great asset that summer.

I didn't know that the Agency of the Year that year, which I had set my sights on,was also known as the Boys Club of Madison Avenue. And I was not a boy named Sue.

I didn't know that an $11,500 starting salary would turn out to be $350 every two weeks, which meant on top of one low-paying job, I needed a few more to make rent.

I didn't know that when I saw Mr. Dusenberry in the elevator and told him he was, indeed, Mr. Dusenberry, and he said, "Please, call me Phil" that I actually would for many, many years.

I didn't know that the boss who promised to help me become a copywriter would be replaced with a boss who didn't believe in promoting secretaries.

I didn't know that out of that frustration I would gain the courage to ask Charlie Miesmer if he would look at my marker-drawn ads (there was no such thing as a Mac) which included a very average campaign for Jelly Bellies – "carry a six-pack in the palm of your hand."

I didn't know much about baseball when I went on my first shoot. At Fenway. With Ted Williams.

I didn't know that Charlie Miesmer, who called me "Kid" for 20 years would hand me the keys to his corner office overlooking Radio City Music Hall when he retired. After all, I still did work at the Boy's Club of Madison Avenue (even though in the late 80s we moved to Sixth Avenue).

I didn't know that the younger people I came in contact with early in my career would go on to be incredible successes in this business. Most impressive, Mssrs. Wall and Graff.

I didn't know people who intimidated me throughout my career would become friends and not just on Facebook.

I didn't know that when I married Joe Credle in 1990, we wouldn't be able to have children.

I didn't know that as a Creative Director, I would channel all those maternal feelings into creating work with other people.

I didn't know working with walking, talking candy for 14 years would be the opposite of a career-killer and that meeting Paul Michaels in 1995 would change my life.

I didn't know when I first used the phrase "What the fuck!" how powerful it could be. But being 5'3, southern and female, I learned pretty quickly.

I didn't know how hard you had to work to be given a nickname by Lubars – Spinney thanks you, D-Tron.

I didn't know when we gave birth to a brand called Cingular in 2000, that we would marry it and bury it in nine years. Nor did I know how emotional that would be.

I didn't know a show called Mad Men would air and a lot of people would think Peggy's character was based on me even though I was learning how to ride a tricycle in the '60s.

I didn't know that in 2012 "Where are the women in advertising?" would still be a headline.

I didn't know that a career in advertising came with the opportunity, and more importantly the responsibility, to do some good in the world.

I didn't know after 24 years at BBDO NY, I would take a plane one way to Chicago to work for Tutssel at Leo Burnett.

And I didn't know that almost every day in this business would make me feel like the first time I walked into an agency. Nervous. Awed. Inspired. Excited. And damn lucky.

So what do I know after 27 years in advertising? Sometimes when you don't know what you are up against, it's harder for it to get in your way.

Jordan Doucette
Executive Creative Director, General Manager
TAXI Canada

Over Jordan's 14 years in the industry, her focus on the success of her clients and colleagues has garnered her a reputation as a valued leader. She has always had a special talent for communicating and collaborating with people and her presence has been a driving force behind campaigns for some of TAXI's biggest clients. Her ability to marry creativity and marketing, paired with her commitment to understanding clients, enables Jordan to translate business challenges into effective creative solutions time after time.

Jordan's work has received awards and accolades from The Cassies, The One Show, The Clios and Cannes.

My First Time

By Jordan Doucette

Give Peas a Chance

That was the first headline I ever wrote. It was on the entrance exam for the post-graduate Media Copywriting program I sort of wanted to get in to.

The pun stated above makes it obvious that my heroes at the time didn't include Bill Bernbach or Lee Clow. Instead, I worshipped Alyssa, my third year University roommate who seemingly had brilliant career ideas. Weekly. Often. Daily. And the passion she had when she spoke of a lifelong career brainstorming ways to sell kitty litter made me believe in her dreams. So much so that I said yes when I was accepted into the copywriting program. Alyssa declined. She, once again, had a better idea.

Three classes later and one used copy of 'Hey Whipple' and I was drawn into advertising like it was the first time I had tasted gummi bears. I couldn't get enough. Suddenly the city full of billboards, transit shelters, radio announcers interrupting silences in cars, shops and homes…it was as though I was seeing and hearing them for the first time. Each one became a billboard advertising my new dream – to become an advertising creative.

I wanted it bad enough that nothing would stop me. Not even the fact that the only car I had to drive the hour and a half to school, was my parents' 'farm' pick-up truck - a truck that smelled like manure even when it was sans-manure. So, add another 15 minutes to the commute since I had to park it 3 lots away from school. You know, just so nobody would see me and confuse me for the small-town girl I really was.

Fast-forward 11 months. I had a portfolio and a dream to trade in that blue pick-up for a city transit pass. I knew it was going to be hard to find my first job. What I didn't know was that finding an internship would be equally difficult. I remember my first interview. They called me.

They. Called. Me.

Said they liked my book, thought I had potential and asked if I could come in to the meet the CD. And I quote, "they would appreciate that." *They* would appreciate that? I wondered if they too were jumping up and down on their Ikea bed squealing at the top of their lungs with sheer excitement.

When I got there to see the CD he asked me why I was wasting his time? He was curious how I managed to find myself sitting in his office. I was surprised he could still see me as I had sunk so deep, deep into the chair I was sitting on the edge of.

But see above…they called me. Which was confusing but also brilliantly clear at the same time. Advertising isn't fair. Or kind. Nor does it adhere to normal workplace sanctioned niceties.

I wanted to cry but I already used up all my energy growing some thicker skin and making a commitment to myself. To not get lost in the sea of 'no' and just say 'yes'. Say yes to the next interview – even if it ends up like the first.

And that's what I did.

I said yes to an internship at a shop that wasn't the hottest in town. But, 12 months later I said yes to a full-time job at that shop. In fact, I said yes with such haste they didn't even get to the part about how much this full-time gig would pay. Remember the truck? At this point, I was considering living in it. But I didn't care, especially when I got my first official brief. To write a car headline announcing its most recent accolade: 'best car in its class.'

Here was the catch. We wouldn't know if the car was actually the winner until the following morning when it was announced in the newspaper. I was to write headlines that evening and have a batch ready for client approval first thing in the morning. I felt like this was my moment. My fate and future in advertising would come down to the brilliance of 7-10 tiny words. I was excited. And terrified. I wrote at least 150 lines but felt none would be good enough.

So can I be honest? I prayed that entire night the car wouldn't win. I actually analyzed the car's features against the competitor's to see if it stood a chance. The differences seemed marginal so I thought I better keep writing. I set my alarm for 4 am to check the newspaper box on the corner of my street. I thought if I could know before the rest of the world, I'd be extra inspired by the win to churn out a few more brilliant ideas. Or if it was a loss, I could crawl back into bed and get some sleep without dreams of cylinders, RPM or torque.

The car won.

They picked one of my headlines.

Other than mine, nobody else's life seemed to have changed. At the time I thought I learned that I shouldn't take everything so seriously. It was just a print ad. Now I realize the lesson was the exact opposite. You never know when a car of the year ad might just turn into the ad that makes your career.

I also learned not all my friends and family wanted a framed copy of my first newspaper ad.

Let's skip the parts in the middle, but saying yes has given me opportunities at the country's best agencies. Working for brilliant minds. It has shown me adventures and opportunities in foreign towns. And speaking of foreign – most recently I've added GM to my ECD title.

Just say yes. Because yes leads to something, which leads to something. And for me, that something has been pretty incredible. Even if, my mother often tells all her friends that her daughter is a very successful photocopier.

Marisa Gallagher
Digital Executive Creative Director
CNN

Marisa Gallagher is executive creative director for CNN Digital. Named to this position in September, 2010, Gallagher is based in CNN's world headquarters in Atlanta and reports directly to KC Estenson, senior vice president and general manager of CNN Digital.

Gallagher runs the experience design practice for CNN across its web, mobile, tablet and other emerging digital platforms. In this role, she leads a team of user experience, video and motion graphics, rich media and visual designers – as they seek to create breakthrough work that makes news and CNN's insightful journalism come alive for people around the world.

Prior to joining CNN, Marisa led the user experience practice for the California offices of Razorfish and served in many other roles during her 10 years there. Before that, she worked in product development at CNET Networks and editorially driven search for LookSmart, a human-powered, human-curated search engine. Gallagher's work in user-centered design has helped organizations as diverse as ESPN, Singapore Airlines, NASA,

McKesson, Visa, Disney World and Cisco to use the digital channel to delight and honor their audiences and customers, while also driving business growth. Gallagher received her bachelor's degree in Anthropology and Film & Media Studies from the University of Notre Dame and an MBA from the University of California, Berkeley Haas School of Business.

My First Time
By Marisa Gallagher

I was wearing a robe.

A plush, velvety number with the lingering smell of lavender that naturally wafts from the comforting threads of spa garb.   For most, it signals a joyous day ahead; of relaxing pampering that brings on a sense of peace and buzzed contentedness to soothe away the rigors of the world.

For me, though, this cape of bliss took on the emotional consistency of a hair shirt; its kind, soft pile gently caressing my skin, agitating me with the unworthiness I felt to wear it. The sparkling-white flip flops on my feet shape-shifted into a sort of jailor's clown shoe, exposing the fake smile of enjoyment plastered to my face. My team and I had collectively waddled to a nearby coffee shop, awaiting the commencement of our day of luxury, and as I sat there, in my terrycloth and plastic glory, awkwardly sipping coffee with folks I'd barely seen out of our hipster south-of-market office space, I just felt ridiculous.

We didn't deserve any of this.

The "team spa day" to a tony spot in Wine Country had been a very kind reward for completing a project – My First project at this amazing digital agency known for innovation and transforming old-school companies like Schwab into new-media powerhouses. Unfortunately, our project wasn't one of those transformational ones; and strangely, being rewarded for it felt oddly patronizing. There's a reason Cannes doesn't give out awards for attendance - it's about more than showing up.

Sure, we'd done our jobs and earned some recognition for completing the work. But it wasn't anything special. It was just a run-of-the-mill, keep-your-head-down, and just-grind-it-out-while-you-waited-for-a-golden-brief type of project. We'd been tasked to help a Top 3 accounting firm "imagine a destination" for its tax accountants working with ex-pats - *and, unfortunately, that didn't mean showcasing the exciting, intimidating, exhilarating, and often confusing life of expats.* It meant creating a way to store a bunch of tax forms and make it feel "sexy." (It was the heady days of the dotcom boom and even accounting firms lost their heads in the rush of it all).

And, we delivered. We presented them with a phone-book-sized deliverable, jam-packed with treatise on "how to write for the web" and "the roadmap for growth"; attempting to arm them with all they needed to make the digital leap and see the potential in connecting their massive network of expat-focused tax accountants. It was solid; a solid six weeks of 9-5 (maybe a couple 9-6's). But we didn't get follow-on work (with the economy starting to turn, hanging out with the *digerati* felt less pressing even to an accounting firm that'd momentarily "gone digital"). We didn't unlock their business or pioneer a new reality for the web, for collaboration, or even for ex-pat related accounting. We just did our jobs; and a nice "thank you" afterward would have sufficed.

But, instead, here we all sat, attempting to revel in the successful completion of this pipsqueak of a project, literally cloaked in inadequacy. We sat together in the "roman baths," bathing suit-clad and warming up enough to make small talk and laugh a bit. Then, we each got to choose treatments from the spa's exhaustive menu of ways to bliss out. The practitioners for my massage and pedicure were highly skilled, yet their touch just reinforced my shame. With each ignoble knot so compassionately released and each common little toe painstakingly coddled, my cheeks burned and my shoulders bowed forward, anticipating prostration before an unknown judge.

But at least I wasn't alone in my shame. Each one of us felt it at least a little and we bonded in our common unworthiness. I, thankfully, was not among douche bags. (Or at least we weren't the kind who felt entitled to spoils beyond our effort). We all had put in a decent days work and were all clearly grateful and appreciative of the surroundings we found ourselves in, though we wanted the bar set higher and to really feel like we struggled and dug deep, climbing heights for such a delicious reward. We wanted to do truly, knock-down, drag-out, I-don't-know-where-that-came-from-but-I'm-glad-it-did, great work. And, when the dotcom bust threw the hammer down on luxury extravagances (and a lot more) a few months later, an odd relief came with it, too. We could finally get down to business and stop parading around as fools.

It was a wonderful gift of a day; for the sweet fleshy indulgences it provided and even more for the drive it unconsciously instilled in all of us. My first project made me feel like a fraud, but almost unknowingly, I've spent more than 10 years proving those first feelings wrong and pushing to turn out work that I feel deeply proud of and blessed to produce. Shame is a strange motivator, though the itch of that kindly hair shirt helps me remember one thing:

we're lucky to do the creative, strategic jobs we do and no sense of entitlement can compete with the rewards that come from truly breakthrough, well-earned, hard work.

Hélène Godin
Executive Creative Vice President, Partner
Sid Lee, Montreal

Meet Hélène Godin, a long time player and contributor to the national and international design scene, in all of its facets. A graduate of the *Université du Québec à Montréal,* she's probably best known for having built her universally recognized multidisciplinary team as well as her insatiable mad love for branding.

Marrying architecture, design and multimedia , she has resulted in stunning environmental and branding revamps such as those for Cirque du Soleil, Société de transport de Montréal (STM), Gaz Metro, the new SAQ stores as well as the urban spa Bota Bota, the latter which recently got her the Gold Lion award at Cannes.

She prides herself on her endless strife to create symmetry among creative disciplines and seeing through projects with an open, integrative approach. Thus, she applied her unique vision through the Sid Lee COLLECTIVE Boot Camp- a multidisciplinary creative incubator that puts eight young, upstart talents to work in solving a pressing business issue for a deserving company.

As a partner at SID LEE, Hélène is no stranger to leading the pack. Guiding one of the world's most highly celebrated creative teams for ten years, she has earned some of design's most prestigious awards including a Gold and Silver Cannes Lion and a One Show Design Pencil award. Her work has been nodded by the Advertising & Design Club, the Type Directors Club, Communication Arts, *Créa* and Grafika. She took part in several juries including the jury for design at Cannes in 2011, CLIO and One Show 2012.

Perhaps, it is her down-to-earth and creative fostering activism for *Héritage Montréal* that sets her apart. Helping to put Montreal on the global map as a truly "design city" has won her recognition in Buenos Aires and Berlin through initiatives with the *Sid Lee Collective* UNESCO city of design. And, frequently giving lectures and spearheading design workshops internationally (such as TMDG in Argentina, *Université du Québec*, Week of Design in Lima Peru, Parsons The New School for Design in NYC and Willem the Kooning in Rotterdam) proves that Hélène Godin can't keep creativity to herself. She knows she was born to share it.

My First Time
By Helene Godin

Making My First Time Last
The first "first" that stands out for me was leafing through my first Graphis magazine, all beautiful and shiny. I wore it threadbare, dog-earing every page. Finally, I had found my true passion.

Then, there was my first apartment that I shared with my sister who was studying architecture: two drafting tables, lots of dirty dishes.

My first day of college, in the Faculty of Design at the *Université du Québec à Montréal*: butterflies. That's where I first met an eccentric Swiss teacher who lived and breathed design. Thanks Mr. Metz; 25 years later, you're still with me.

My first creative workshop: Ontario Street, with a bunch of other fanatical design students. There were 11 of us crammed into one apartment. Gabriel listened to Barbara; Diane and I listened to Brel. There was always a lot going on, including occasional schoolwork.

My first love.

My first design pay cheque: $500. Who knew you could actually get paid for this? I quit my part-time job. I felt like a million bucks, and I thought: "Hey, why not go to Switzerland?"

My first portfolio, 100% hand-made, held together by super glue and a few panic attacks. It's still intact. It got me that internship in Switzerland.

My first experience living in a commune, with a bunch of would-be anarchists in Switzerland: I learned very little about design, but a lot about life.

My first "break & enter" at a Swiss poster warehouse (with those anarchists again): that's how I started my poster collection.

My first "real" job was in an exhibit-design office. Today they call it "experiential design" and "storytelling." Back then, we were just designing exhibits. It was a tough learning curve, especially when they told me I had to negotiate prices with our suppliers (big mistake).

My first love, again.

My first near-heart-attack: a Letraset typo on dozens of ready-to-go documents. Total humiliation. More proof that designers can't spell.

My first Mac on my first day at Cossette – the ultimate communications agency: very intimidating, sweaty palms… They put me in a hallway where advertising and design kingpins would gawk at me as they passed by. I was the newbie – and scared shitless.

My first business trip: I went to Vegas with my boss to present the poster for the Cirque du Soleil show *O*. I felt like "Captain Quebec" trying to conquer America.

Everyone was incredibly nervous, including the clients. The walk through the hallways to get to the meeting took longer than the presentation itself. Steve Wynn came in, with reporters and dog in tow, and instantly declared it "a real piece of art." What a circus!

My first hire happened after I was named Co-Creative Director. I saw it as a huge responsibility, and I got hugely lucky. I hired Yann Mooney, who remains my faithful partner in crime.

My first meeting with Philippe Meunier, co-founder of Sid Lee, was in a café. Magic happened. After 11 years of dedicated service to Cossette, I was ready for a change, ready to become Creative Director. As usual, I got by on a combination of nerves and chutzpah.

The first time I made partner was on a road-trip to Charlevoix with our Chairman, Bertrand Cesvet. We were meeting a Cirque du Soleil co-founder for an ambitious new project. Bertrand's car skidded into a snow bank, so we had to take a bus back home. I figured I had him cornered, and I told him he'd be crazy not to make me partner. He looked at me and said: "You're right." Nerves and chutzpah pay off once again. I think the recognition was more precious to me than the partnership itself.

Our first "Agency of the Year" Award: after recognition for me, recognition for my firm. Sweet. And it got sweeter and sweeter the second and third times.
My first TMDG conference: speaking in Argentina, in front of 6,000 young South American designers. Magical moment – I felt like a rock star.

My first Cannes jury: very glam.

My first Sid Lee Boot Camp, in 2011: an insanely intense "creativity incubator," a project invented out of thin air with Philippe and my colleagues. I actually recaptured the spirit and energy of that Ontario Street apartment – and that's saying a lot. Only at Sid Lee.

My first presentation for the (RED) Foundation, Bono's organization, for our 2012 Boot Camp: once again, I felt like a rock star (and so did Bono, I assume).

And now, my first time writing about my first times.

I guess what I'm trying to say is, the key to creativity is always putting yourself in a "first time" situation. Yes, it makes for a rather nerve-racking existence, but nobody said creativity was a walk in the park. It's a journey filled with countless first steps.

One day, maybe, I'll feel like I've arrived and I'll want to rest on my laurels a bit. That would certainly be a first.

Janet Guillet
Executive Creative Director
DDB/NY

I am lucky. In life. And in work.
I love what I do and I'm lucky to be good at it.
I was "born" at DDB. Left twice and came back twice.

The first time I left to write a screenplay, which I entered into a Writer's Guild competition, and landed in the top ten out of 800 submissions. (Sadly it never got produced. Long, heartbreaking story for another time.) The second time I left to head up a small Miami shop called HMS Partners. Six months in they sold the shop and the focus was no longer creative.

Back to NY and DDB, where over the years I've headed up Exxon Mobil, Amana Appliances, Hershey, Merck, Transitions Optical and Georgia Pacific.
I love to pitch and win business and I'm good at both.

Words I live by: "Life's too short to work with assholes." And happy to report I haven't had to work with too many.

My father wasn't one to give advice, but when I was graduating high school and not sure what I wanted to do, he said: "Just pick something you like doing because you'll be doing it for a long time."

Thanks Dad.

My First Time
By Janet Guillet

When I graduated from School of Visual Arts in the 80's, I made a list of agencies I wanted to work for. DDB was at the very top. I got hired and, though I left and came back twice, I've pretty much been here ever since.

When I first got here there were so many talented women in senior positions. Diane Rothchild, Jane Talcott, Deanna Cohen, Patty Volk--not to mention the mother of us all, Phyllis Robinson, who had just penned the "You. Only Better." campaign for Clairol. Women worked on everything: Chivas Regal, IBM, Volkswagen, American Airlines.

It was about the work and the best work was rewarded.

But then something changed. The work that was being rewarded.

I think the Super Bowl changed advertising for women. I throw it out there knowing that women are sensitive to being accused of whining. This isn't whining (see, still sensitive) it's just an observation with some heavy-handed generalization.

When the Super Bowl became the "Oscars" of advertising, the accounts and products that were most coveted were those advertised to men. This begat the era of frat house humor. Horses farting, men getting kicked in the nuts, three stooges type of stuff. I remember my partner, Marcia Murray, and I being briefed on the Bud Light "Great Lengths" campaign for the Superbowl. We just kept thinking, OK men go to great lengths for a *domestic light beer*. They come up with excuses NOT to be with hot women just to have a *domestic light beer*. A beer so ubiquitous you could grab one at any bodega or quicki-mart on the interstate. Needless to say our ideas didn't make it in. But any time one of those spots came on, my husband would guffaw, yes, guffaw!

And then something else happened. Most of the judges judging the work were also men (still not whining, just observing) so there became a similarity in the type of humor that was being rewarded.

And then the men that did that type of stuff got promoted and became our bosses!

The good news is I do believe it's changing. I was not a judge at Cannes this year, but had I been, the Chipotle "Back to the Start" film would have also been my choice for the Grand Prix. Perfection. And not a farting explosion in sight.

Getting back to my first time. My boss was Dianne Rothchild. To this day, I owe any success I've had to her. She was my mentor. Smart, funny, ambitious. My partner and I were fresh out of art school, where all our projects where juicy, fun and big, and here we were being asked to do a trade ad for Cigna Insurance. Actually, *Re-Insurance*, which to this day, I'm still not exactly sure what it is. I know it has something to do with insuring really big things, like factories and power plants. So day after day we struggled trying to do award-winning work. The kind of work that got us our jobs. Work that would win us praises. Book-worthy work!

And day after day Dianne rejected ad after ad gently redirecting us each time. Finally she said: "Guys, stop trying to win awards. If you just solve the problem in a clear and intelligent way, chances are you will win an award."

So we sat there and stared at each other for days. Then called the account person to come tell us the story about reinsurance again. And she said, "Guys, imagine that you own a factory, and there's an explosion and all that's left is rubble. Then you find out your insurance company doesn't have the money to pay the claim. That's what re-insurance does, it's like the back up to the main insurance."

Then we finally saw it. A factory in ruins, still smoldering, and the line: A Disaster is about to Happen.

If we did that ad today, we would do a stock search and have the perfect image in about 3 seconds. But since this was before computers and the internet (it shocks me to even read that line) it wasn't so easy. So we had a model maker build us a miniature burned down factory, singed oil drums and all. It was perfect. And Dianne was right. We won a Clio for that very ad.

A funny add to that is that my Mom proceeded to tell everyone she knew that I one THE Clio. As if there was only one and I got it. I have to admit it sounded better than winning in the Business to Business Single Page Trade category.

Susan Hoffman
Partner, Co-Executive Creative Director
Wieden & Kennedy, Portland

One of our few Portland natives, Susan Hoffman started her career as an art director at Pihas, Schmidt, Westerdahl before moving to TBWA\Chiat\Day in Seattle. Three years later she came to Wieden+Kennedy as employee No. 8 and has spent the last 27 years defining the agency's culture and setting the bar for creative excellence.

Susan has a tendency to shake things up a bit. That's probably because she finds the status quo boring. Case in point, a walk past the Dakota building in New York City inspired her choice of The Beatles song "Revolution" for the Nike spot of the same name. She's injected her unique perspective into some of the most memorable ads W+K has produced for virtually every client we've ever had. Susan is never satisfied unless the work feels fresh and interesting.

Since David Kennedy's "retirement" in 1993, Susan has provided the visual yin to Dan Wieden's storytelling yang. She's worked as a creative director, opened both our Amsterdam and London offices, serving both as executive creative director, and ran Wieden+Kennedy 12, our experimental ad school. Along the way she's introduced the world to directors like David Fincher and Michael Bay and helped launch the careers of many of the most successful creative directors in the industry.

In her current role as executive creative director of the flagship office, she's tasked with preserving what makes this agency special, continuing to nurture the creative talent within our walls and pushing forward to find new and different ways of working and thinking.

My First Time
By Susan Hoffman

My first commercial was for NIKE. It was called "The Shooter", for boys' basketball shoes. I was the art director and Jim Riswold was the writer.

I naively remember when we sent the boards out, how excited all the production companies were about the idea. Now realizing they just wanted the work, good or bad.

We were clueless if it was good or not, but it made us feel great.

So we had an approved concept, hired the director, and headed to LA for the shoot.

But when we arrived for the pre-pro, we found out the idea had already been done.

Our creative directors were Dan and David and they said we needed to quickly re-concept the spot because the airdates couldn't change and we had to stick with the shoot schedule.

So we walled ourselves up in our depressing hotel room and called Dan/David every hour with new ideas (mind you this was back in 1985 when even fax machines weren't invented!)

And in the early years of WK we didn't stay at nice hotels. We stayed at this dump off of Franklin that was so bad, that on another shoot for Kink Radio, the client called me and said she was too scared to stay in the hotel. So it wasn't like Jim and I were sitting by the pool lapping up the sun as we merrily re-concepted.

I just emailed Jim and asked him the name of the place and I quote him: "I remember getting stuck in the same room of that place with Wieden. He can snore with the best of them. In fact, he can suck the paint off the walls with his snoring. I, thankfully, cannot remember the name of the place." Oh well.

Another classic Riswold story from the shoot was that he had barely stepped out of Seattle, Washington. Portland, Oregon was a big move for him; so going to LA was like an international city. And he brought traveler checks!

So here we were walled up in the scary hotel sending ideas to Dan/David. The account person, Kelly Stout, had also flown down with us and later that day, when she saw how desperate we were, she started throwing in her own ideas.

She had one idea that we begrudgingly thought was OK, quickly called Dan/David, they approved it and that was the spot we produced. But you can't appreciate it until you see it. Probably the worst ad done at WK!

Here's the link:

http://wk.wiredrive.com/l/p/?presentation=e125edc9c5630160d0da4d1108 f31285

Julia Hoffmann
Creative Director
Department of Advertising and Graphic Design
The Museum of Modern Art, New York

Julia Hoffmann is the Creative Director of Advertising and Graphic Design at The Museum of Modern Art in New York where she oversees brand identity and design for exhibition graphics, advertising, signage, and collateral projects for all of MoMA's exhibitions and programs. She leads a creative team to develop design solutions that enhance MoMA's brand in New York City and around the world.

Previously Julia was an interactive art director at the Colorado-based advertising agency Crispin Porter + Bogusky, where she worked for clients such as Burger King, Microsoft, and Volkswagen. She started her career working for Stephen Doyle and later for Paula Scher at Pentagram in New York, where she designed identities and branding systems, packaging, and publication design for clients including the Public Theater, TIME magazine and The Metropolitan Opera in New York. She was the lead designer on the award-winning bestseller The Daily Show with Jon

Stewart Presents America (the Book): A Citizen's Guide to Democracy Inaction.

Born in Frankfurt, Germany, Julia earned her BFA from New York's School of Visual Arts, where she now teaches.

My First Time
By Julia Hoffmann

It was two years out of school, while working at Pentagram, when I was assigned my first big project.

It was a book for Jon Stewart, an American comedian, who has a very popular American late night satirical news show. The brief was to design a book he and some of his writers were writing about America, in the style of a mock American history textbook.

There were quite a few problems with me on this assignment, which nobody seemed to notice or be bothered by, such as:

- I didn't really know who Jon Stewart was because I didn't have cable TV.
- I grew up in Germany so I had never been exposed to an American textbook...on top of that I went to a "weird" school where, believe it or not, we did not use textbooks.
- Although my English was decent, I lacked the cultural references/nuances needed to understand most of the jokes. To put it simply, at that time I could not really understand what's so funny about Seinfeld.
- Finally, I had no clue about American history...did I mention I grew up in Germany?

So, here I am, designing a book that has almost 20 jokes per page, written by one of the funniest comedians in America, and I could not get half of the jokes.

It's also worth highlighting that this was also my first time meeting/working with a client. Prior to that I would just do the work and my boss would be the one meeting and presenting it to the client (sometimes I would go along but I would not say a word). To say I was nervous would be an understatement. Therefore, to "protect" myself, I projected a serious demeanor which I felt would be the best way of showcasing my professionalism, so I did not crack a smile for the first two weeks (I was also a little lost with the subject matter and the jokes).

I think this was driving them (Jon and the team) a little crazy, they are comedians after all and here's the German designer who won't laugh (pretty stereotypical).

Anyway, the project quickly grew into something quite massive in scale (240+ pages) and this being my first time I decided to give my all to it – I had to make a great impression!

The pace was pretty crazy and all consuming. It went a little something like this: The writers would send their chapter once a week; I would then put the text into layouts, side tables and charts. I would also comb through all of their jokes and design a layout for each which would then be sent back to them. Of course, once graphically exhibited they would realize that some of the jokes would not make sense so we would have to start over. All of this for three months that seemed like a very long all-nighter. I really gave it my all, this project became my life for those 90 days I worked on it.

Also in these 240 pages, every other page had some illustration or chart. This being my first time, and not knowing better, I quickly blew the illustration budget by commissioning two well-known German illustrators to do 3 spreads. This left me with all the other illustrations to do myself which was a blessing in disguise, since I discovered my love for making charts and illustrations.

It was the best *first project* to jump into, to learn graphic design, illustration, dealing with a demanding client and project management.

I learned how to push myself to the limits and last but not least actually learn about American history. I realized that you can use graphic design to transcend language.

And in the end, I finally got some of Jon's jokes.

I am trying to have *first times* as often as possible, because first times are to some extent safe. You are expected to fail or you have beginner's luck. It seems a win win situation. The side effect is that you are learning something new.

Rachel Howald
Chief Creative Officer
WPP/Team BAC

Rachel Howald is currently the Chief Creative Officer for Team BAC/WPP where she oversees the global Bank of America brand portfolio.

Her brand and agency experience include the following: Executive Creative Director at mcgarrybowen, running the Chase and Marriot International brand portfolios; Global Creative Director on Intel, Holiday Inn, and Staples at McCann NY; Founding Partner of Howald & Kalam, a creative boutique whose clients included Intel, Nokia, Genworth Financial, and thestreet.com; and Group Creative Director at Y&R New York on Genworth Financial, Computer Associates, Weight Watchers, and the Wildlife Conservation Society. Her career began at DDB NY, where she went from Junior Copywriter to Associate Creative Director in 18 months. Client experience includes NY Lottery, Bermuda Tourism, United Airlines, Princess Hotels, AT&T, Verizon, Gilda's Club, Hersheys, Johnson & Johnson, Amtrak, General Mills, and Kraft.

In addition to being one of the youngest people ever named to Crains Top 40 Under 40, her accolades include an Emmy nomination, recognition in every major advertising awards show, and her work is part of the permanent collection of the Museum of Modern Art. She has also served as a judge for the One Show, New York Festivals, and AICP show. A graduate of Oberlin College with an M.A. from the University of Texas, she is actively involved in advertising education, having served as a guest lecturer at Miami Ad School, Portfolio Center, and UT-Austin, as well as Executive-In-Residence at the University of Oregon. She is an advisor to the board of the National Master Chorale and Women for Women International and a member of the board of the Fisher Ensemble.

Her greatest source of pride is her two sons Callum and William, whom she and her spouse Jennifer happily shuttle around New Jersey in a minivan.

My First Time
By Rachel Howald

" 'Stop sleeping with my husband.' the note said. And she did. Until she realized the note wasn't from his wife. It was from a nosy copywriter on the sixteenth floor."

That's the first paragraph of the novel I'll never write.

Nelson Stuart is the name of the first patient whose knee I won't reconstruct after he tears his ACL going for a layup.

And Myrna Smith is the name of the first woman I won't be representing as a hard working but scrappy junior D.A.

Why? Because I didn't fulfill my third grade dream of becoming an author. Or my high school dream of becoming an orthopedic surgeon. Or my college fantasy of becoming a lawyer.

I went into advertising and became a creative.

The first assignment I had was an agency-funded half page ad in the back of a program congratulating a senior exec at DDB on her selection as a YWCA Woman Achiever. In other words, it was a complete throw away that was a perfect junior assignment because there was no actual budget, no real client, and nothing at all on the line. I didn't know that at the time. I just knew it was MY assignment and there was nothing more important in the world.

There was very little time (there never is) and there was only a tiny budget for stock art, time permitting. My art director, Lara Gilmore, and I toiled away all day, coming up with idea after idea. Our creative director, Jane Talcott, said she would review them at the end of the day because the ad had to be released by 5pm the following afternoon. We proudly pinned them to the wall. She gave them the once over and then said the worst thing any CD can say. They were "okay." "Okay?" Tantamount to "eh." Code for "If only there were trained monkeys here who could randomly type something good." We were crushed. We were inspired. We were destined to stay up all night trying to come up with something better.

The next morning, there we were again. A little less eager to pin work up, but a little more confident that these were better. We pinned. She looked. And there it was again. "This one is okay." Only now we were out of time. This piece of okayness needed to be produced to get out the door by 5. I don't remember what it said. Something about little girls in China. Why would I remember it? It was only okay.

We dragged our dejected selves back to my office and decided to damn the torpedoes and keep writing. We worked all morning and into the afternoon. At 3pm, we went back to Jane's office. We didn't even have time to pin. We handed over the pile. She looked. We waited. And there, toward the bottom of the pile, was more than an okay. There was an actual smile and a "Fucking fantastic!" followed by a "You have 90 minutes to comp this up and get it out the door. Go! Go!"

It made it (just barely) to the people printing the booklet for the luncheon. It made it to the wall of the agency for a month. And it made it to the Art Director's Annual where it won a Silver even though it was just a nine word white headline on black (in Copperplate…it was the early 90's): "Success is the one thing no woman can fake." (still true, by the way).

Winning the award was nice. But honestly, it wouldn't have mattered. Because I had found a job that paid me to think and write and create and get paid for doing what, to this day, I'd be doing for free anyway, just for fun.

It's nothing I ever dreamed of doing, but I can't imagine doing anything else. I'm not alone in that. In all my time in the business, I have yet to meet anyone who's said "When did I decide to go into advertising? When I was 3, I said to my mom. "Screw being a cowboy or a policeman or an astronaut. What I really want to do is creative direct."

Advertising is like love. You fall into it. One day, you don't even know it exists. And the next, you wouldn't know how to live without it.

If you too are lucky enough to land a career where you can wear (insert your choice of casual clothing and footwear here), where you get to travel around the world to places most people only dream of, where you're surrounded by fascinating (albeit occasionally certifiably crazy) people, and where clients will spend hundreds of thousands if not millions of dollars turning a random thought that passed through your brain into advertising that is seen by millions of people, then you are not just lucky. You, my friend, are downright blessed.

Sure, there will be long nights and weekends and frustration and disappointment and not a single thing you ever produce will be as perfect as it was when it was just an idea in your head. And you'll kvetch and rant from the rooftops about the grave injustice of something that did or didn't happen the way you thought it should--until you hear yourself talking and remember that there are plenty of people working hard at real jobs and you're not one of them.

Because most days will be other days—unbelievable days--where the nice lady from the test kitchen shows up at your office door with 6 flavors of pudding for you to try. Or you get flown in a helicopter to a research facility to watch a robot arm test dish soap by systematically scrubbing scientifically baked-on spaghetti sauce off a lasagna pan.

You'll discuss five year old boy Batman Halloween costumes with Stefi Graf while you're shooting at a fifteen million dollar compound in Las Vegas, steps away from the pool house where the Rat Pack used to gather in the summer.

You'll travel to Palm Desert in 104 degree heat and meet a hundred year old African-American woman whose grandmother was a slave and you'll see her eyes light up when she talks about this new young presidential candidate, Barack Obama.

You'll wander down a cobblestone alley in Paris and eat one of the best meals of your life in a place that you'll swear was also probably a brothel.

You'll get that first One Show pencil you lusted for but you won't care because your pregnant partner will be sitting with you, 2 months shy of delivering your first son and your only thought will be "When is this show going to end? I don't want to be out too late." And then you'll bring that son to L.A. when he's 19 months old and you get nominated for an Emmy and the whole night, your only thought will be "When is this show going to end? I don't want to be out too late."

And every day, you'll go into work knowing that you'll never be bored. You'll always be working on something new and different. You'll always be learning random facts you never knew about hotel remotes or life insurance or toilet paper or trains or chocolate bars or airlines or zit cream or multi-million dollar enterprise management software. And along the way, you'll be learning more about yourself.

And every time will feel like the first time.

PS: My only words of advice: Don't be an asshole. To anyone. Not the security guard. Not the cleaning lady. Not the client or the CEO. And don't tolerate people who are. Oh, and sign up for the 401(k).

Judy John
Chief Executive Officer, Chief Creative Officer
Leo Burnett Canada

Three years into the business, Judy John was ranked Canada's 'Top Copywriter' in *Strategy's Creative Report Card*. Judy's resume reads as a who's who of top Canadian advertising agencies, ranging from the small, creative independents to the large multinationals. In addition to founding her own agency, Guerrilla TV, she has worked at Chiat/Day, TAXI, Roche Macaulay & Partners, BBDO and Ogilvy & Mather. Judy joined Leo Burnett Toronto in 1999, as Chief Creative Officer and in 2011, added CEO to her title.

Under her direction, Leo Burnett Toronto has been recognized nationally and globally, winning at virtually every show. Highlights include winning the first-ever D&AD Black Pencil in the Digital category, creating the most awarded billboard campaign in the world in 2009, introducing James Ready Beer to the world, and being the most awarded Canadian agency at the One Show in 2011 and then again in 2012 -- winning 9 pencils across all four shows: One Show, Design, Interactive and Entertainment.

Judy was ranked the #1 creative director in Canada in *Strategy Magazine's Creative Report Card* 2010 and 2012 and the agency was ranked #1 in

2012.

Everything from Judy's work ethic to her management style, she learned from years of packing take-out orders at her parents' restaurant.

My First Time
By Judy John

My first ad landed me a cushy job and a staff of 8. I didn't know what I was doing but isn't that true of a lot of first time creative directors?

The ad (actually, a campaign because it ran in different colors) was a poster running for high school student council. I think the headline was: Vote for Judy John for Publicity Director. Or something clever like that. I know it must have been clever because I won. With a staff armed with Bristol board and colored markers, we were responsible for advertising all the school dances, bake sales and other epic events. I lead my team to such memorable, and since copied, ads as: 'Bake Sale tomorrow in the main hall. Noon. Be there.'

Truth be told, I didn't recognize this as an early discovery of my passion, I joined student council to get out of class. I was an academic slacker. I picked publicity director because the other council positions seemed like a lot more work and besides I loved watching TV and I'd seen a lot of ads. I didn't inherit the Chinese work ethic, despite my tiger-like mom's efforts making me work at our family restaurant at the age of 8.

For years, I'd discounted my successful run as Publicity Director. It was during an alcohol filled university school trip to Daytona Beach when I had one of those drunken 'What the hell am I doing in film and theatre. I don't love it the way these nerd do. What do I love?' revelations.

When I got back, I started applying to advertising programs.

What I learned: Everyone is good at something. Don't take it for granted, do what you're good at.

Cut to two and a half years later.

My roommate served drinks at the Four Seasons pool where a creative team, Stephen St. Clair and Jeff Odiorne, went to work all the time. Without this introduction, I still might be a security guard working the

95

pizza hospitality tent. The team got me into the small agency they were working at, where I spent the summer writing research papers on cooking oils. When they moved to Chiat/Day Toronto, they set me up with an interview with their creative director, Joe Alexander. I had never heard of the agency or Joe. To say my school left me ill prepared would be an understatement. I didn't have a portfolio and worse yet, I didn't know I needed one.

What I learned: If people like you, they will help you.

The interview couldn't have been more than 15 minutes. I followed Joe as he walked through the creative department, stopping as he checked up on teams. He walked quickly, so I was always a few feet behind him. Every once in a while he would turn around and fire a question my way.

Joe: Did you bring your book?

Me: Um, no? What book?

Joe: Your portfolio.

Me: I don't have one.

Joe: Have you looked at the One Show or Communication Arts?

Me: What? Uh, no. Not yet.

I could feel his disappointment as he realized I was wasting his time, so I started to sell. I told him I needed an internship to graduate so I was free labor for 4 months. I was willing to do anything: get coffee, run errands, work in any department. I was eager and willing to learn. I think he felt sorry for me, with no book and no chance in hell of getting an internship anywhere else. And I think Stephen and Jeff must have told him what an awesome research paper writer I was. I became Chiat/Day Toronto's first intern.

What I learned: People will help you but you also have to help yourself. Research the agency you're interviewing at. If you're too dumb to do that, look pathetic but somewhat useful.

I spent 7 weeks of my internship in print production: organizing the proof room and getting mechanicals signed. I got to know everyone in the agency and what they did. I offered to help anyone who needed it. I went to every party. Then I spent my last 6 weeks in creative, four of those weeks filing for the creative assistant, who had an even more dubious work ethic than I did. I spent every weekend working on my book and showed my ads to anyone at the agency who would see them. Because of my new found work ethic, I got offered two full time jobs at the agency, one in print production and the other as copy editor. Despite the lure of a full time job, and with the encouragement of some of the creatives that I could make it as a copywriter, I turned down both jobs and continued to work on my book, every night and weekend.

What I learned: Be useful and work your ass off.

With a few weeks left in my internship, Stephen asked me if I wanted to work on an ad with him while Jeff was on holiday. It was a brief for an in-store poster and brochure for Nissan's warranty. I didn't sleep that week. 'How to back up a car.' was my first real, published ad. It ended up getting in the One Show.

As luck would have it, towards the end of my internship, they were looking to hire a junior creative team. Joe had left, and Marty Cooke joined the agency as CD. I thought Marty had no idea who I was until one day he came by my cubicle and said he'd heard he should see my book before hiring a copywriter. When he offered me the job, he said there were so many people in the agency rooting for me, I would be his most popular hire.

What I learned: If you work your ass off, good things will happen

I attribute my success as an intern, and my entire career, to the work ethic and attitude my parents' instilled in me when I worked at the restaurant. 'Work hard and be nice to people,' is what I hear in my head to this day. That and 'Why don't you dress nicer?'

I've found over the years, it's hard to find good interns. Some get it, some just don't. To help increase their chance of success, I hand them a sheet with pointers when they start: How to turn an internship into a job. Given they have some natural talent and follow my 10 tips, they should be able to land a job in advertising and / or a restaurant.

Margaret Johnson
Executive Creative Director, Associate Partner
Goodby Silverstein & Partners

After graduating from the University of North Carolina at Chapel Hill with a BA in journalism and mass communication, Margaret took a hard right and pursued an art direction degree at the Portfolio Center in Atlanta, GA. Her first job was freelancing for a small advertising agency in Providence, Rhode Island called Leonard, Monahan, Lubars & Kelly where she cut her teeth on accounts like Polaroid and Keds tennis shoes.

A few months later, she decided to pack up and head for the Lone Star State. She took a job at The Richards Group in Dallas, Texas where she worked on Id Software, creators of video games like "Doom" and "Quake." She launched lots of games with imagery of monsters, screaming faces and dead bodies. She also produced work for Continental Airlines and Humvee (you know, Arnold Schwarzenegger drives one).

A couple years later, she received a call from Goodby, Silverstein & Partners in San Francisco. She packed up and headed west again. In twelve years, she's worked on just about every account in the building– Sonic,

Häagen-Dazs, Logitech, Nintendo, Specialized, hp, Foster Farms and Budweiser, just to name a few.

When she's not working, she enjoys running, kickboxing, movies and traveling. In 2008 she completed her first film, Dunkumentary, which was part of the Short Film Corner at Cannes.

My First Time

By Margaret Johnson

It was June 6, 1996. I had made it. All the way from my tiny cubicle in Dallas, TX, to San Francisco, to the office of Rich Silverstein. *The* Rich Silverstein.

The office was immaculate: a drafting table, a phone and hundreds of books perfectly arranged by subject (art, cars, architecture, etc.). He stormed in, gruff and mustachioed, with the air of a New Yorker born and raised.

"Let's see it," he said, and started flipping through my book. He was looking at the ads, then up at me, then back at the ads, then back at me. He made his way through the portfolio and then paused at one ad in particular. It was my hero piece, an ad that I had done for Continental Airlines when they were sponsoring the Woodstock music festival's comeback. It featured a Boeing 737 wrapped with peace symbols, flowers and psychedelics.

I was sure he was pausing to say he had seen it in *Communication Arts* (my first appearance in *CA*!). He frisbeed the laminated ad across the room.

He started in: the retouching was terrible, and it was obvious that we had faked the wrap on the plane. I tried to explain that we were on a budget and that we turned the ad around in two days. He didn't care. "When someone's flipping through a magazine, they can't hear your excuses." The interview was over.

The next time I saw Rich Silverstein was about a month later. Incredibly, I had gotten hired, but had been coming to work every day and posting up at my desk largely unnoticed for two weeks. I went up to his office to ask for an assignment. He looked up and saw me. Long, awkward pause. It dawned on me: he had no memory of our interview. I landed an assignment, but I left that office absolutely certain that I had been hired by mistake.

Two months later, I finally met Jeff Goodby. He was tall and had a ponytail and wore Birkenstocks. He seemed very California, even though I learned that he grew up in Rhode Island and went to Harvard. Jeff had an assignment for me. A friend of his at KGO Radio had called in a favor. He needed a billboard campaign for their game-day broadcasts of the 49ers' games.

I wanted to use a jersey as a backdrop, with the headline lettering made to look like the players' names on pro uniforms. It was a hard thing to make look authentic in Photoshop, so I decided to have real letters made out of felt. I found a seamstress who said she could do it and turn it around in time for our shoot.

When I went to pick the letters up, I was horrified. She had cut them out by hand with what must have been extremely dull hedge clippers. The letters were jagged and had strings hanging off them. They looked like someone's four-year-old daughter had cut them. I panicked.

We shot the jersey that day, got an engraver to help out with the retouching work and made the mechanicals. I was relieved—they looked fine. The billboards went up all over San Francisco. The day the billboards went up, I got a call from Jeff's assistant asking me to come up to his office. I walked in expecting to be congratulated on a job well done on my first big assignment. The conversation went like this:

Jeff: I was driving in this morning and I saw those billboards you did.
Me: Oh, cool!
Jeff: Yeah, um, not so cool. Those things are really hard to read. I mean, it's the smallest type I've ever seen on a billboard. Seriously, it looks like legal mouse type or something…my wife was with me, and she couldn't even tell who they were for.

Me: Oh, no.

Jeff: So what do you think we should do about this?

Me: Fix it?

Jeff: That's going to cost a lot of money.

Me: You can have my next paycheck.

I survived the billboard debacle (Jeff picked up the repair tab), and sixteen years later I'm still at GSP. As I was putting this story together, I asked Rich about our first meeting. He doesn't dispute that he'd forgotten who I was. But he surprised me by reeling off the contents of my portfolio in detail:

"These aggressive ads for Hummer SUVs— distressed typography, over-the-top headlines paired with killer shots of trucks kicking up dirt. Then, there were those video-game ads for *Doom* and *Quake*. Page after page filled with grenades, guns and faces screaming in agony," he laughed. "This tiny little girl with a Southern accent...and a book full of testosterone."

I know that sixteen years anywhere is a freakishly long time in this business. I like to think that I'm still here for one reason: because I found the rare place where they may forget your face, and may forget your name—but they don't forget the work.

Laura Jordan-Bambach
Creative Director
Dare, London

As Creative Director at Dare, Laura brings together an experimental and innovative use of technological advances and digital media with a deep understanding of changing customer behavior and good ol' fashioned storytelling.

A Creative who has worked internationally (Australia, Japan, United Kingdom and the United States) producing content which pushes the boundaries of the medium, Laura cut her teeth as a key figure in the infamous 'geekgirl' hyperzine in the early nineties, and has been involved ever since in the design and implementation of many of the world's most cutting edge work for top international brands as diverse as Levi's®, Mini, Bacardi, SAB Miller, BT, COI, Barclays and Virgin Atlantic.

She has consistently won awards for her commercial work, and has been honoured with personal recognition over 15 years in the industry, including being voted one of the 30 under 30 leaders in IT by industry leaders as part of the Fairfax Group awards, and recently the New Media Age Greatest Individual Contribution to the Industry Award in 2011.

After a stint as a lead creative at deepend Sydney, she arrived in London for the deepend head office in 2001, and has worked at a senior level at Lateral, I-D Media London, glueisobar and LBi, before coming to Dare in 2012 to help shape the agency of the future.

She lectures and travels extensively, speaking on experiential/digitally-connected art and the cultural implications of digital society, as well as teaching dynamic lectures and workshops around new forms of communication and marketing, advertising, innovation and digital narratives in classes at major Universities and centres of excellence (including Hyper Island, School of Communication Arts 2.0, College of Fine Arts Sydney and the RCA).

Laura Jordan-Bambach acted as a jury member for many awards, including:
D&AD Black Pencil judging
D&AD Student Awards
One Show Interactive Awards
Creative Review Annual
Creative Showcase
Creative Circle
Eurobest
Cristal Festival Awards
International Ferstival of Media Awards Grand Jury
BIMA
FWA

She is also co-founder and Director of SheSays – an international volunteer organization to encourage more women to take up digital creative careers, which operates in 12 cities worldwide. She is a trained taxidermist, and believes in the power of great ideas, grown through focused collaboration, to create great work. She believes that genuinely entertaining or useful is where it's at (at least most of the time).

My First Time
By Laura Jordan-Bambach

"Here Comes Your Man"*

In 1991, I was the passenger in an old clapped-out Honda Civic, with my mate, Shan Chan at the wheel. Our Pixies mixtape was at full-volume on the stereo. We'd driven from Sydney's rural outskirts and we were on a mission. To understand my entry into advertising I guess I need to start from here.

We were on our way to enrol in a summer-break art course at the College of Fine Arts in Sydney. I was 17, and desperate to go to art school to follow my passion. I was going to do something creative with my life (damnit!) and was completely obsessed with making things in a way that only someone of 17 can be.

Passing through central Sydney that morning, a billboard done as an art project by Australian collective <u>VNS Matrix</u> became my inspiration, my epiphany and driving force, my mission and my sense of purpose for the next 22 years. A Cyber Femminist Manifesto for the 21st Century.

The following year, I found myself stepping again into COFA, this time as an undergrad. THE JOY! The billboard had opened up a world of possibilities to me around gender politics, philosophy, 'the abject' and technology, and so with that in mind I threw myself wholeheartedly into both the most cerebral and visceral ends of the Fine Arts curriculum. And as 'multimedia' (as digital was then called) sat in the Photomedia department (photography, plus computers) where I majored I also threw myself into coding, designing and animating everything I could, 24/7. This, I thought, was what I was built to do. This was FUN.

It was in 1995 that my commercial career and Very First Time sprung up out of a chance encounter with one of my cyberfem heroines – Rosie X (@rosiex) from *geekgirl*, a new 'zine (and website) that had launched to showcase women in technology (thinking, doing, researching).

I'd been to Rosie's magazine launch at the bookstore next to uni, and was totally in awe of both her drive and ambition. I bought her magazine and her stickers: "Put Down That Pony and Pick Up a Computer" and "Girls Need Modems".

By this stage I was creating a lot of 'net art' and interactive installation work myself at COFA – learning new technologies as they rapidly appeared on the scene and spending all my time in the computer labs hanging out with the technicians (I was one of only two students of my year to specialise in digital rather than photographic art). My room was full of kit from floor to ceiling. Even the end of my bed was covered with electronics.

And this is where serendipity kicks in. I sold vintage clothes at the local markets every Saturday, and one very hot day around Christmas 1994 Rosie X had her own stall there, selling her 'zine and paraphernalia. The conversation went something like this:

ROSIE: Is that a tattoo of a web on your stomach?

ME: Yes, it's an Escher – an infinite tessellation of spiders.

ROSIE: Could we take a photo of it for the back cover of the next issue of *geekgirl*?

ME: HELL YES! Here's my number, and email address.

Weeks later and I get the call that was to be the definitive start point in my "industry" career:

ROSIE: Bad news, the photographer has pulled out, so we'll have to cancel.

ME: I do photography at uni, I can do it!

ROSIE: Um, ok. Also, the designer doing the cover has pulled out so I'm thinking of postponing the issue.

ME: I can use Photoshop, I'll design the cover for you!

ROSIE: Ok. Can you code? Because I need someone to help on the website, too…

And so it was that I became an Art Director, without ever having learned (at that stage) typography, layout or even that you DON'T REALLY USE PHOTOSHOP FOR PRINT WORK. I look back on that first cover and its utterly terrible, but full of love.

Rosie and *geekgirl* gave me an outlet for everything I went on to learn – from Flash and Director to more complex HTML coding even before WYSIWYG interfaces were invented. Yes, I coded in Notepad and even learnt PERL.

And because of the passion ignited in me in 1991 I had one thing on my mind, to try to connect with other creative women working in technology at the birth of the consumer web. It gave my creativity an outlet and my discoveries a purpose, and incredible opportunities to travel the world showcasing both our work and our opinions. Part adventurer and part artist, realising that I was both loving the geekery and was pretty good at it, too.

So it started, the "industry" found me and I became a professional Creative. In 1996, while working on my Masters, I set up my own company, "Joystick Digital Media", working on advertising, design and digital systems, mostly direct with clients through word of mouth or *geekgirl* contacts. My agency work was *myspecial*, I was the secret fixer of projects for bigger agencies around Sydney, who had bitten off more digital than they could chew with their own clients. I'd come in, code what needed to be coded and correct designs where it was needed. I'd upload files to servers and reduce file sizes from the insanely huge documents the agencies print designers had mocked up, to something what worked. I'd teach how to animate GIFS and explain what a CGI script was. I'd sleep on the floor to hit their deadline 72 hours later, then take a week off (playing Marathon after hours, and drinking copious amounts of instant coffee).

"WHAT FUN" I thought.

I made websites for cereal brands and the navy, and animations for the local school. By 1998, I was a Creative Director running a team of designers, developers and content folk transitioning magazines to the web and teaching others the magic of this new medium.

And how did I end up in London? That's a whole other story involving a man in a skirt, a rock star and a portfolio that took me 100 hours to make in Flash 4. I'm still passionate about women and technology though, and I still wake up every morning thinking WHAT FUN!

When I was 8, Dad gave me a sticker that read "sometimes the best man for the job is a woman". It stuck. Thanks Dad, this is for you.

Linda Kaplan Thaler
Chairman
Publicis Kaplan Thaler, New York

Linda Kaplan Thaler is responsible for some of America's most famous, relevant and touching advertising campaigns in the industry, including the Aflac duck quack heard round the world and the daring "Yes, Yes, Yes" for Clairol Herbal Essences. Much of her work has become part of the American pop-culture landscape. She has authored and composed campaign jingles that are among the industry's gold standard. Some examples are: "I Don't Wanna Grow Up, I'm a Toys 'R' Us Kid" (Toys 'R' Us); "Kodak Moments" (Eastman Kodak) and "The Heart of Communication" (Bell Atlantic). Of her 13 Clio Awards, two were for Best Original Music and Lyrics.

Today, Linda is the Chairman of Publicis Kaplan Thaler, a fully integrated advertising agency with digital, social and technology at its core. The agency is the U.S. flagship within the Publicis Worldwide Network, and its blue-chip client roster includes: P&G, CITI, Nestle, L'Oreal, Merck, Pfizer, and Wendy's, among many others. Previously, Linda was CEO and Chief Creative Officer of the Kaplan Thaler Group, which she founded in 1997 and grew from a fledgling start-up to a company with over a billion dollars in billings. In July of this year, the Kaplan Thaler Group merged with Publicis New York to form Publicis Kaplan Thaler.

Linda is also a best-selling author and television personality. Her three collaborations with coauthor Robin Koval have all received national recognition. Their most recent title, *The Power of Small: Why Little Things Make All the Difference,* debuted as an instant national bestseller. Linda and Robin's previous book, *The Power of Nice: How to Conquer the Business World with Kindness*, debuted on the *New York Times* and *Wall Street Journal* bestseller lists. *Bang! Getting Your Message Heard in a Noisy World*, a savvy marketing book and their first title, was also a national bestseller.

In 2005, Linda hosted the Oxygen television series "Making It Big," where young professionals competed for their dream job. To launch the show, Linda starred in a series of promotional commercials, which received the 2006 American Women in Television & Radio Gracie Allen Award for Outstanding Commercial Campaign. She has also appeared on Donald Trump's "The Apprentice" as a judge.

In addition to her Clio awards, Linda's creative talents have earned her the prestigious New York Women in Communications Matrix Award, the Advertising Woman of the Year Award from Advertising Women of New York, the UJA's Mac Dane Humanitarian Award, the Women's Leadership Exchange's Compass Award and the Girl Scout's Woman of Distinction Award. Most recently, Linda was presented with a New York Women in Film and Television's Muse Award, the first woman in advertising to receive this honor.

A native New Yorker, Linda was a Phi Beta Kappa and Magna cum Laude graduate of CCNY, with a bachelor's degree in psychology and a master's degree in music. Linda currently sits on the Advisory Council for *The Colin Powell Center* at CCNY and previously served as the 2010/2011 President of New York Women in Communications. Linda is married to composer Fred Thaler and has two children, Michael and Emily.

My First Time
By Linda Kaplan Thaler

My first time was with Dick Van Dyke. It was thrilling, it was new, it was exhilarating. But it was also a bit anticlimactic. I shall explain.

You see, umpteen years ago (you didn't think I'd be giving away my age this early in the story, did you?), I started my first day of my advertising career at J. Walter Thompson (before they even abbreviated their name). The agency had been trying to sell Kodak a TV spot for their Colorburst Cameras for months and couldn't make the sale.

When I was assigned to the project, my mind started racing. Clearly, the client didn't love the work. But there must be something he *does* love. Aha – animals. Cute animals. I mean, who doesn't love those?

Dogs? Too common. Kittens? Too allergic. I know, how about *dolphins*? They're so smart and shiny and happy! (And the perfectly natural choice for a Bronx native like me).

Dick Van Dyke, who was widely popular at the time, had already been booked to star in the Kodak commercials. So I thought, how about Mr. Van Dyke taking a picture of a dolphin? Capturing that one moment when he flies into the air, that burst of energy and fun!

I took pen to paper and wrote some clever copy (or at least I thought it was at the time). And guess what?

Turns out the client LOVED dolphins! Who knew? Much to the surprise -- and chagrin-- of the other writers working tirelessly on the account, I sold my first national TV spot after less than one month in the business.

Of course, the agency considered it verboten for someone as low as me on the totem pole to attend the shoot. But even though I never got to meet

Flipper or Dick, I'm happy to say that the final commercial was pretty cute. And it was set to air just a few weeks later.

A dear friend (Laurie Garnier, alias Laurie Birnbaum at the time) invited me over to watch the spot, and we celebrated with champagne and cake.

I called my parents as soon as it ran. My father – always one of my biggest champions and honest critics – said, "Well, it was a nice commercial, but not as funny as the ones with James Garner for Polaroid." Thanks, Pop.

At work the next day, my creative director told me that, although I loved the spot, a year later it would no longer even be on my reel. And he was right about that. I was fortunate enough to work on many brands and myriad commercials over the next umpteen years (see, I'm still not telling you my age).

So what did I learn from my first time?
Don't be afraid to jump in feet-first, get wet, and, just maybe, make a big splash. After all, it worked for Flipper and me.

And, who knows, you might one day find yourself with a lovely, albeit faded, Kodak memory of your own.

(Speaking of Kodak memories, my other "first time" was with an unemployed Trotskyite who had just graduated from Columbia with a degree in "Overthrowing Democracy." I wisely decided not to call my dad afterwards. I mean, if he didn't even like Dick Van Dyke.)

Margaret Keene
Executive Creative Director
Saatchi & Saatchi, L.A.

Forget the Love Boat and Charlie's Angels, as a kid I loved the commercials. In 1993 I found Chiat/Day and turned my love into a full blown obsession.

I was taught by the best in the business. As Lee Clow's assistant and art director, I worked on Apple and won my first awards working on "Think different."

One of my greatest achievements was creating The Pedigree Adoption Drive and Foundation with my partner Chris Adams. A global initiative, activated in 27 countries, donating millions of dollars to shelter dogs in need.

In 2010 our team set a new course for the Nissan brand with "Innovation for All" and engineered the first ever iAd on the iPhone for The Nissan Leaf.

In 2011, I became Co-ECD of Saatchi & Saatchi, L.A and have had the privilege to work on the Toyota brand.

I've enjoyed working on some of the most successful national and global brands in our industry. Some awards include Cannes Lions, Communication Arts, D&AD, The One Show, The $100,000 Grand Kelly (donated to The Pedigree Adoption Drive), Obies (two Best of Shows), The New York Art Director's Club (Best of Show), and multiple Effie Awards including three gold, bronze global but my single greatest accomplishment is my amazing family.

My First Time
By Margaret Keene

I always wanted to make commercials. Between episodes of *Bewitched* and *Iron Eyes Cody* tearing up over litterbugs, I knew it was the only thing I ever really wanted to do. I'd realize later it was the only thing I could do; but that's a whole 'nother story.

During the late eighties, I saw a video of strange looking dude, long beard, glasses, denim shirt, showing some storyboards to some very uptight businessmen. He was unflappable and totally mesmerizing. And although his enthusiasm didn't seem to rub off on the suits, they did seem to be caught up in his spell. I'd learn later that those men were Porsche clients and the bearded guy was Lee Clow. When I saw that video, I knew I would work for Lee and I spent the next few years working my way up from my little white Aaron Brothers art table in my doublewide mobile home, to the desk of Lee Clow at Chiat/Day Inc.

I played it cool most days. There were too many folks wanting his attention so I acted like I was totally content to answer his calls and book travel; but at night I'd hijack someone's computer and try in vain to create something that could somehow compete with the radical creativity that was happening there at that time.

One day I answered a call from a guy named Steve. I sort of begged him for his last name and he curtly replied, "Jobs." What happened then was nuts. Lee and Steve were back together again and the rebirth of Apple was underway. Lee was always a believer that great ideas came from anywhere and so he let lots of us take a crack at the campaign. "Think Different." had many cooks but Lee was the visionary. He knew what it needed to be even before anyone started concepting.

My buddy, Jessica Schulman, and I tried adding interesting women. Quick, try naming ten historically significant women, pre-Internet. Kind of tough, right? We went through every woman in every periodical we had. We even looked in the dictionary and there it was, a photo, *the* photo, of Rosa Parks. That was it! But not just as an outdoor board - Rosa was on a bus so of course her image should wrap the bus. (It feels so good when an idea just clicks. It's stupid how simple it is. And honestly, it never happened for me that easily ever again).

Steve bought it and Lee was proud. Jobs flew me up to The Apple Campus and commissioned a special bus commemorating The Rosa Parks Foundation. He ushered everybody to the front of the campus to check it out. He was so stoked when he saw it that he ordered fifty more right there on the spot. I won a bunch of big awards and Lee finally made me a junior art director. This was it. I made it.

A couple weeks later I was given my first big assignment, a third page Winter Olympics ad in TV Guide. What? Third page, TV GUIDE?! Try putting two Eastern European surnames on a third page ad. Shit. Yes, every junior has to start at the beginning but boy did it hurt.

Over the years I worked long and hard to make it back onto the Apple team and went on to create lots of cool stuff. But in retrospect, I was incredibly naïve, mildly talented and irritatingly persistent. I never realized how long it would be before I actually knew what I was doing and how hard it was going to be to get there.

And to be honest, I'm so glad that Lee never told me.

Janet Kestin

Co-founder of Swim

Janet Kestin was Co-Chief Creative Officer of Ogilvy Toronto before founding Swim, a creative leadership lab, with long-time partner Nancy Vonk in 2011.

They have won many top industry awards including Cannes Lions, One Show Pencils and Clios. They are the creative directors of Dove "Evolution", winner of two Grand Prix at Cannes, and "Diamond Shreddies, winner of a Grand Clio.

Janet has judged many of the world's top advertising awards shows including Cannes, Clios, One Show and D&AD.

Janet and Nancy's honors include being named to Creativity magazine's Top 50 creative people of '08, advertising Women of the Year at the WIN Awards in LA and the AWNY Awards in NY in '07, and induction into Canada's Marketing Hall of Legends in '11.

Janet is a mentor and frequent lecturer at universities and ad schools including the renowned VCU Brandcenter.

Their widely read advice column, "Ask Jancy" on ad site ihaveanidea.org spawned critically acclaimed Adweek book, "Pick Me", in 2005. It has become a staple in advertising schools from Texas to Turkey. They are currently writing a business book for HarperCollins.

My First Time (ish)
By Janet Kestin

PROLOGUE
Co-worker: So, what does your wife do for a living?
My husband: She writes ads.
Co-worker: You mean someone actually writes those things?

LOGUE (cute, I know)
Over the last few weeks, I've overturned drawers, ransacked closets, and conducted an archaeological dig of my basement in an attempt to unearth the earliest evidence of my ad career. Eureka. A cracked, dusty, black portfolio peeks out from behind a pile of unused lumber, old stereo equipment, a couple of broken lamps, several tubs of childhood memorabilia and the box from a 20-year old Cuisinart. You can see how often I go down there.

The portfolio feels suspiciously light as I yank on the uncooperative zipper. A few sheets of yellowed paper slide out. Are they my first?

(Cue the wavy lines)

On that day, long ago, when I was riding the Montreal metro trying to decide what to do with my life, I didn't even know that advertising was a job. All I knew was that I was a pretty good writer and it was the only thing anyone might pay me for. I'd applied to newspapers (remember them?), magazines, television and radio stations. I was coming from an interview that didn't look all that promising, staring blankly at the mostly crap posters that run along the upper edge of subway cars. I thought ,"I could do better than that." Light bulb.

I went through the Yellow Pages. Called every ad agency in Montreal in alphabetical order to find out what I needed to do to apply for a job. I was all the way to "Y" before anyone agreed to talk to me. After showing me some of the work and delivering a mini-lecture on the business of advertising, the Creative Director of Y&R Montreal told me that if I wanted to work in advertising, I should "put together a book and stop dressing like a nun."

I didn't really know what a "book" was, but I'd seen a few nuns in my time and as far as I could tell none of them ever wore a red turtleneck dress. The whole experience was baffling. I holed up in my living room and wrote lines like "Butter makes a batter better". Ouch. My first crack at a portfolio had headlines so pun-filled that I'd fire myself in a second. Still, someone kinder than me gave me a shot. Before I knew it, I was writing - you guessed it -credit card statement stuffers in prose so compelling that within weeks, I was promoted to writing inspirational matchbook covers for the Four Seasons hotel. "A night of perfect sleep is as rare as a perfect diamond, and more to be desired." You know the type of thing I mean. I toiled in my cubby, praying for a few fewer editor's red marks on my copy, my very own art director and and waiting for my big break.

I wish I could show you what it looked like when it came. It was a TV commercial for a dessert called Pudding in a Cloud- chocolate Jello pudding sitting on a cloud of Cool Whip. I was working with an art director for the first time. A very senior, very British, eccentric, artist-fashion photographer-film director-art director, obsessed with big blue skies and clouds. "Pudding in a Cloud" was a natural fit, I guess. My art director was many brilliant things, but he wasn't a teacher. I did what I was told: *read the brief, go to the meeting, try not to put your inexperienced foot in your mouth, keep it simple, keep it short, write it again, write it again, write it again, if there's nothing to say, sing it, find a voice that's memorable, try to say something intelligent, but not so intelligent that no one will understand it.* I wrote a simple set of lyrics about the floating dessert. The account guys wanted them changed. The clients wanted them changed again. The evolution of the storyboard. The endless tinkering. The art director-fashion photographer-film director. The editor cutting, splicing. The first music track, the second, the third.

122

If you work really hard, I'll bet you can imagine the heavenly blue sky, clouds drifting lazily across it, Pudding In A Cloud drifting equally lazily. I kid you not. That partnership didn't last. He wasn't a partnership sort of guy.

First-ish ad. Hopefully worst ad.

EPILOGUE

When I first noticed posters on the subway, I figured any idiot could come up with work like that. By the time I'd actually finished my first real ad, I figured that no matter how bad it was, you deserved a Cannes Lion just for surviving the process.

At the end of my first year in my first real partnership, we were doing an inventory of what we'd accomplished. All we had to show for our blood, sweat and tears (mine), was four pieces of paper. One of them fell out of that old, cracked portfolio.

It was for Toro lawnmowers, which offered a technology that was new and different for its time.

The headline was "This is the only time you'll ever see a Toro broken down." It was an intelligent dissection of the lawnmower. It was no Cannes Lion, but it was no Pudding In A Cloud, either.

Joyce King Thomas
Former Chief Creative Officer
McCann, New York

Joyce King Thomas is best known as the writer behind MasterCard's "Priceless" campaign, which runs in 100 countries and has been spoofed by everyone from Ralph Nader to Bart Simpson. During a 17-year tenure that saw her rise to Chief Creative Officer of McCann Erickson NY, the NY agency won over a billion dollars in new business and created iconic ideas like the Staples Easy Button campaign which went beyond an ad campaign to become Staples' best -selling product.

She has won numerous awards and served as a judge in the industry's most prestigious award shows, including Cannes, the One Show and the Clios.

Ms. Thomas is currently a partner at Longreads, the social reading site that New York Magazine calls "highbrow and brilliant." She also serves on the board of the Nurse Family Partnership, a group that teaches parenting skills to young mothers living in poverty.

My First Time
By Joyce King Thomas

"I bet your mother loves this portfolio."

It was 1977. I had rotary-dialed from a payphone on Madison Avenue to the office of the creative recruiter at Doyle Dane Bernbach, and he had agreed to see me. I was 21, fresh from Missouri, naïve blue eyes beneath gigantic glasses, L'eggs pantyhose peeking out of a pair of high-heeled sandals, which were all the more ridiculous because it was December. And snowing. And Manhattan. My Queens cousin Francine had accompanied me to the city and the recruiter insisted that instead of waiting in the lobby she should come into the interview as well. That should have been my first clue.

After flipping through the ads I had written for my college newspaper, he looked at me and said those words: "I bet your mother loves this portfolio."

It was my first and worst day in advertising.

I didn't end up getting a job in New York that December. My university had produced renowned journalists, but hadn't yet become a great school for advertising. My portfolio showed it. So I had to start a little south of my goal.

I worked my way from a recruitment advertising agency in St. Louis, Missouri to a quirky little shop in Tulsa, Oklahoma to the Wells Rich Greene office in Dallas, Texas where I wrote the first ad that made a real difference in my life: the ad that got me a copywriting job in New York.

It began the way most ads begin. Parity product. Standard brief. Writer staring at blank piece of paper. Writer staring at art director staring back at

126

writer. We tried puns. We tried clever visuals. We tried puns with clever visuals with palm trees in them.

After a couple of days we did what creative teams the world over have done when faced with a hard assignment. (Or perhaps I should say, we did what creative teams have done when faced with a hard assignment and the bar down the street is closed.) We got mad. We yelled at the account people. We railed against the client. We hated our job. We bickered with each other. We ripped up the brief and tossed it in the garbage.

All this activity seemed to get our endorphins flowing and we began to get somewhere.

We set out to learn more about the product we were trying to sell. This was before the days when you simply typed the client's name into the Google search bar. Learning more about the product meant reading annual reports and brochures and anything else you could get your actual 3-D hands on.

And amidst all that dull material, there it was: the truth. A perfect little truth just sat there saying, "use me". This fact made flying our client's airline a no brainer. We crafted the simplest of ads around this irresistible reality. The ad didn't need elaborate artwork or a photograph of a palm tree (alas), just a simple graphic to make our point.

My creative director was happy. The client was happy. Even the managing director of the agency was happy.

The ad was not a Cannes Lion winner. Honestly, I can't even remember the headline. But we had outsmarted the brief and uncovered a really good reason to fly the airline. When I asked to be transferred to NYC a couple months later, the agency said yes. Pretty soon I was living in the city that had worked me over but good three winters before. Not only that, I was walking down the same halls as legends like Mary Wells, Charlie Moss, Bob Wilvers and Paul Margulies.

And my mother loved it.

Sasha Koren
Global Interactive Creative Director
Avon Products, Inc.

Sasha Koren is the Global Interactive Creative Director of Avon Products, Inc., a company that has empowered and inspired women for more than 125 years. She is responsible for formulating a creative vision to connect the extensive network of independent local markets, as well as for developing and executing strategic digital tools (web, social and mobile) to support the businesses of more than 6 million Avon Representatives worldwide.

Sasha joined Avon after an award-winning, 20-year career on the agency side, having led the interactive creative teams at top advertising agencies Arnold Worldwide and Kirshenbaum Bond & Partners, as well as pure-play interactive shops R/GA and Organic Inc. She has a BFA in Graphic Design from the Rhode Island School of Design.

Sasha's work has been featured extensively in design annuals and magazines, has garnered many design and advertising awards, and has smashed industry averages for advertising response rates. She's made beauty and fashion an area of specialty with clients such as Revlon, Levi

Strauss, Redken, Coach, John Frieda & Bioré. Other key client relationships include Hershey's, Bank of America, Brooklyn Academy of Music, Beech-Nut and Glaxo Smith Kline; among many others.

In her spare time, Sasha is the brand creative director and one of the founding organizers for FIGMENT Project, a non-profit association created to build community through free, volunteer-run, participatory arts events around the world. A third-generation New Yorker, Sasha lives in Hell's Kitchen with her husband and daughter.

My First Time
By Sasha Koren

This was my first serious job out of school. My dream job. I'd wanted to work at R/GA from the moment I graduated but they didn't have a position available, so I had to wait an entire year. When they eventually called, I was the very first interactive hire in the Design Department. Of course there were other designers (working on motion graphics, special effects and print) but I was the first one hired to focus solely on interactive. I had no idea at the time what a big deal this would turn out to be.

I also had no idea what was actually expected of me. Nor did I know what it meant to work for *The Legendary Bob Greenberg*. All I knew was that I was in awe of my two Creative Directors, John DiRe and Jakob Trollbäck; and the enormity of their design talent was so completely overwhelming that every day I just focused on coming in and doing whatever I was told.

Shortly after joining the company we had a big deal client buzzing around the office: Courtney Sale Ross. She was a personal friend of Bob's and someone who moved in his elite social circle. She was not only high energy, but also insanely wealthy and she left a whirlwind (and many new projects) in her wake.

Courtney was the recent widow of Steve Ross (the mastermind behind the Time Warner merger) and she had founded a new school. Actually, to call it just "a school" would be a gross understatement. At the time, the jury was still out on whether she was a nut or an educational visionary, but she was attempting to completely overhaul the way children were taught.

The school would be a private incubator for learning in the 21st century! With a bleeding-edge technological infrastructure to support a network of schools from East Hampton to China! It would have a new educational model, which would better prepare students for a modern, globalized future! Courtney had incorporated the latest progressive teaching methods from brilliant Harvard educators, and had even hired a noted cultural historian to design a completely unique (and *extremely* elaborate) "Spiral Curriculum" which promised to encompass the history of civilization across all cultures.

Somehow, despite my obvious inexperience, I ended up as the lead designer for The Ross School's very first website.

It was a crazy project that went on forever—in part because we had an entire team of genius CGI computer animators rendering and re-rendering visualizations for the school's Spiral Curriculum. First it was rendered with lines. Then with mist. Then with tubes that intersected to create an 8-part, multicolor, flower-shaped core. It radiated smoke, had dust particles and thumbnails of student art projects orbiting each curve, and had a huge beam of light that shot up through the middle illuminating it from the inside out. The visualization was not only complicated, but every detail represented a deeply significant, mission-critical, educational philosophy and had to be faithfully integrated into the website.

As a 23-year-old graphic designer in my first serious job, this spiral was the absolute bane of my existence. It's all very interesting to talk about. But it was VERY painful to try to bring to life as the centerpiece of a high profile website that had to have a lot of actual information on it. Like THE ADDRESS OF THE SCHOOL or how to apply for admission.

For months I went around in circles with that stupid spiral trying to make it work. Spiral in the middle. Spiral cropped. Spiral big. Spiral solid. Spiral misty. Each design was progressively weirder and more pie-in-the-sky than the last, and I just couldn't find a way to put all the required elements together on one screen.

Eventually, time ran out. Courtney would be coming in from East Hampton with her entourage to see her new website, and Bob Greenberg would personally make the presentation. And I had nothing. Call it writer's block for website design, whatever. I was blank.

But the strangest thing was that even then, I couldn't seem to get anyone's attention. John and Jakob were both focused on the infinitely more important motion graphics work that was on their plates, and while they would throw me the occasional offhanded suggestion for a book to look at, it was clear that no one was going to sit with me and show me how to save this project.

So with only the weekend left, it was up to me alone to pull it all together—and I resolved to sit in the office until I nailed it! And I did sit in the office. But I was so utterly lost that I spent the entire weekend playing computer games. Occasionally I'd move the spiral to the left or to the right, but mostly I just sat there, eating up the time. I knew that if I could only demonstrate just HOW stuck I really was, prove to John and Jakob that I really had tried, that they would finally come to help me.

I think I logged 90 hours that week, most of it on the weekend. And I gladly put it on my timesheet to show that *"I was there."* That *"I was trying."* Of course I had no idea what timesheets were really for, I just wanted John and Jakob to know that I was there, trying to do *something*.

But things didn't go exactly as expected... First of all, I didn't count on being confronted after the weekend about why I billed so much time. I was horrified (and completely freaked out) to learn that working longer hours was not actually better!

But even worse was the sobering fact that I STILL couldn't get John or Jakob's attention. No one assessed my status on Monday. No one looked at my work. And no one sat with me to help me pull it all together!

Time ticked by and still nothing... Monday became Tuesday, and the presentation was Friday afternoon.

Finally, on Wednesday, I was hit with the realization that Bob was *actually* going to present this freaky abomination to Courtney. And worse, that the infinitely talented John and Jakob, not to mention the brilliant CGI guys, would all be there to watch me let them down—to watch me fail.

Thankfully, that didn't happen. In my 11th hour panic, when I finally let go my expectations of being saved, The Ross School site came pouring out of me.

The interface turned out to be groundbreaking. Simple technology was transformed into an entirely unique visual design concept. Sliding shoji screens mirrored the architectural design of the school and referenced its focus on globalism. Visitors were enticed to playfully explore the information, discovering hidden quotations from important people along the way. And on every page, a different slice of the spiral peeked through, guiding the eye and gluing everything together.

I remember sitting alone at my desk during the presentation, too low on the totem pole to be invited, wishing I could see Courtney's reaction. Momentarily John returned to the design studio to get something left behind, and as he passed my desk he put his hand on my shoulder, smiled and said, "You really did a great job, Sasha. I'm proud of you."

As I look back, I am so grateful that I was left to flounder, and that no one realized I needed saving. Because that Wednesday, much to my surprise, I figured out how to save myself.

I had no idea that during all that time procrastinating, all that time feeling paralyzed, I was also percolating with ideas. And it turns out that during that weekend playing video games, *I actually was there*. And *I actually was working*.

Over the years I've gotten much faster, and I can to tap into the final creative vision earlier, without panic. But this experience taught me that "focused down-time" is actually a critical part of my creative process. In fact, I've learned that my best work almost always happens in the background, subconsciously. And I have learned to trust that even when I'm not actively doing it, I'm still doing it.

The Ross School site won many awards for R/GA and went on to be published in books and magazines for years afterwards. And while I can only imagine how many redesigns and iterations of the site they've been through in the 20 years since it first launched, they're still using the shoji screen concept today.

Natalie Lam
Executive Creative Director
McCann, New York

Natalie is executive creative director at McCann Erickson New York, leading the transformation of the agency and heading up integrated work for global brands such as IKEA, Nespresso and L'Oreal.

Prior to McCann, Natalie spent three years in China as executive creative director running OgilvyOne and building brands for clients like adidas, Chanel, Vans, Johnnie Walker. With her leadership OgilvyOne Shanghai was one of the most award-winning integrated/digital agencies in Asia.

Before China, she was creative director at R/GA New York, leading the Nike+, Nike Running and NIKEiD accounts. She was part of the original small crew that created Nike+, and launched the first global Nike Human Race in 2008.

Lam's work has picked up an ADC Gold Cube, Cannes Titanium Grand Prix, D&AD Black Pencil, One Show Interactive Best of Show and Grand Clio. She is a frequent jury member of industry awards, most recently as Interactive Jury Chair for the Art Directors Club.

My First Time
By Natalie Lam

I've been very lucky so far in life, getting my first job was fairly smooth, even though I didn't know anything back then.

In 1992 I moved alone from Hong Kong to New York for art school. I spent my first year at Parsons and found it too restrictive. So I moved to Cooper Union where I sampled a little bit of everything: photography, printmaking, design, typography, and film. This was where I got away with a drawing as a final project in a Math class. I loved the freedom of living in New York but had no idea what I'd do when I graduate. Cooper was a place for dreamers, unlike Parsons which was a place for go-getters. A girl a year older than me in Parson returned to Hong Kong and became the most popular singer and actress, to this date.

I didn't want to return to Hong Kong.

It was a tradition for seniors at Cooper Union to have a graduate show, I showed a bit of typography work. Before the show ended I got two interview calls: one from a Robert Wong of Frankfurt Balkind Partners, another from a startup called IO/360.

Without a proper job placement advice department (or maybe I was too dumb to seek it out) at Cooper Union, I only knew that I must get a visa to stay in NY.

Much later on, I found out Frankfurt Balkind specialized in award-winning annual reports. IO/360 was a web design startup (one of the first back in 1996) by Cooper Union graduates just a couple of years ahead of me.

I picked Frankfurt Balkind simply because they had sponsored foreign visas before. I didn't know what else to ask for, including what the hell the agency does.

I started working in the Fall. Fall/winters were busy seasons for annual report design firms since they needed to go to press around January.

Between September and January, from assisting senior designers, sitting in internal presentations, dealing with the print production department, I vaguely learned the process of creating annual reports over many endless nights.

I learned that Frankfurt Balkind is more than just a design firm. It understood the differentiation between one Fortune 500 company and another; and crafted beautiful, provocative stories that summed up what each company did every year. In the early 90s the Wall Street Journal did a story on a genre-defying annual report with a lime green cover for Time Warner—that was Frankfurt Balkind.

But the irony was, regardless of the story, the beautiful design and art direction, the size of the printing budget, the number of gloss vs matte varnishes, the many hours we spent getting rid of dust and spots on the print proofs, whether we were being innovative and conscious by using soy-based inks, when the shareholders received the annual reports, the first thing they did was to tear out the story-telling pages, and keep the financial charts.

All this was new and overwhelming to a naïve 22-year-old who spent 16 hours everyday indoors in the cold winter. 90% of the time I watched and learned, 10% of the time I relied on my instincts. Things were pretty smooth; knowing that I would get kicked out of the country if my visa lapsed because I got fired also helped.

In early February when the season came to an end, all the senior designers went on-press and the agency was quiet. One day, the big boss, Aubrey Balkind, came down to my empty floor looking around for people.

In my five months there the longest conversation between Aubrey and me was "Hi." Aubrey was a respected but feared character. To me he looked like a more intelligent Mr. Burns, Homer Simpson's boss. He had a raspy voice that didn't help the intimidating factor.

I tried to look down and not be noticed even though I was the only person sitting on an empty floor. My heart was beating fast.

Aubrey walked by my desk, asked me if I could work on an annual report with a three-week turnaround, all by myself. Normally an annual report took 3 to 5 months, with a team of senior designers, copywriters, junior designers, and production crew. I didn't know I could've said "no".

The back-story: It was a new client. They had spent four months with another design firm and killed it last minute. They came to Aubrey for a brand new direction that need to go to press in three weeks—otherwise the annual report wouldn't be printed in time for SEC filing which was against the law.

I practiced everything I knew: keep it simple; don't do anything that makes you look like a fool. I had another rule: focus on one thing I want to explore with each assignment to keep myself interested.

The client was a car parts manufacturer from the South. Every art school student at one point or another was fascinated with line art illustrations and that was my thing at that moment. I designed the whole annual report in the style of instruction manuals with line art illustrations. Very art-student-y, but the clients bought it, probably out of time, pressure and we couldn't afford photo shoots. I made the CEO's portrait in the style of an illustrated a drivers' license, thinking that made perfect sense.

It was a lean team. I wrote the story, did all the illustrations; Aubrey edited the client-supplied copy, with an account director and another respected but feared production head Tina Moskin, all of whom weren't too happy about the impossible timeframe.

I applied everything I learned to this, not knowing if I was doing the right or wrong thing at any moment. I just knew that I had to keep going. I learned to sneakily push boundaries by slipping things past Tina's watchful eye.

Besides almost getting caught by Tina a few times, and not knowing exactly what Aubrey had in mind most of the time, everything was fairly smooth. Until one day I missed a major deadline; so we had to specially courier the layout at 4am for it to reach the client by 9 the next morning. That cost more than $300 instead of the regular $30 by Fedex—I made $1,200 a month pre-tax.

At 4am, a very angry account director called me from home.

Feeling utterly helpless and alone in the cold dark office with no other soul around, I cried for the first time in 4 years since moving to New York. I don't cry easily; my friends always said I'm a guy who wears the pants. Between then and now I've only cried one other time while watching this amazing Brazilian movie *Central Station* in the late 90s.

I swore never to cry again because of work.

That was the best lesson I've ever learned.

I'm extremely thankful I learned that lesson so early, and Aubrey giving me such an incredible opportunity. I think I learned 80% of what I know today from 16 years ago.

My current boss Linus Karlsson said it well: your success depends on your first boss. I was lucky I learned a lot in my first time.

Epilogue:
Aubrey sold Frankfurt Balkind to Hill Holiday.
Robert Wong is now CCO of Google Creative Labs.

I/O 360 went public after one year, all the founders retired by 1998. Tina is still feared and loved by many.

Alessandra Lariu

CEO, shout
Co-Founder, SheSays

Ale Lariu is the CEO of shout (everybodyshout.com) and co-founder of SheSays (weareshesays.com) a five year old award-winning global network organization focused on the engagement, education and advancement of women in digital marketing.

In 2010, Ale was picked by Fast Company magazine as number 29 out of the 100 most creative people in business beating Tom Ford, Jamie Oliver and the founder of FourSquare. In 2011 she was elected 'World's Most Influential Female Creative Director' by Adwomen and got an award for 'Greatest Individual Contribution to New Media' by NMA magazine. In 2012 she was in FastCompany's "League of extraordinary women" with 60 other amazing ladies like Hillary Clinton, Oprah and the founder of Kiva.

Ale has been kicking ass for as long as she can remember. Before starting her own company, she was SVP Group Creative Director at McCann, where she has worked with clients like MasterCard, General Mills, Kohls, Nikon and Verizon. Before that, she worked for Agency Republic, a digital boutique shop four times best interactive agency in the UK. Her 15 year-old career in advertising has lead to 18 prestigious industry accolades including Cannes, D&AD and OneShow. She also spoke at over 15 conferences in the past five years.

Ale is a guest teacher at Hyper Island (Sweden), Berghs (Sweden), Miami Ad School (NY) and Boulder Digital Works. She presented at Wharton and Columbia University. She also writes a monthly column on digital culture for the Brazilian version of Wired magazine and is on the board of the Art Directors Club and the Creative Review Board for The Ad Council.

Ale was born in the Brazilian Amazon jungle. She grew up in Rio de Janeiro and in 1994 was awarded a scholarship from the Brazilian government to do an MA in London where she lived and worked for 13 years before moving to the US. She speaks five languages but mixes them a lot.

My First Time
By Alessandra Lariu

The art of not knowing and other experiments

Warning: I'm going to start off brief. But don't blame me, blame technology. I started working in digital when sites were rare. CD-ROMS were the only thing available then.

And I was taking what I could get.

My relationship with work started in 1995. I was fresh from an MA in "Electronic Publishing" - no one knew what to call digital then, Laura Jordan-Bambach will agree with me here - and I very geekily taught myself how to code HTML, Lingo (a dead programming language now) and how to use Photoshop. We were not just producing messages to communicate products and services, we were making the products we wanted to advertise. Something that I hear is very in vogue right now.

In 1995 I was interning (read photocopying) for a company producing CD-ROMs in Basingstoke, 40 minutes from London. They had just finished an interactive guide to London and were getting ready for a Paris version.

I asked if I could get a job on the Paris CD and they asked me for a resume. At lunch time, when everyone was away, I used the boss's computer and put one together. I wrote I could design and program. I could also speak French and had extensive knowledge of Paris, as I lived there when I was 15. All true, except for the fact that my expertise was only around the 9th *arrondissement* where I lived for a couple of months.

They bought it and I got a job as a producer and interactive designer. Interactive jobs were scarce then, so you had to try different things and master multiple skills.

145

Advertising didn't know about digital and vice-versa, as digital wasn't part of culture as it is today. And don't even mention YouTube - that only came about ten years later in 2005 as a very bad dating site. But 1995 was exciting for me, it was a time for a lot of unknowns and experimentation. People were supportive and trusted you to do your thing, unlike some of the (how shall I put it?) more precious people I met when I joined the world of advertising.

For the Paris CD-ROM I was also the only art director, even though I didn't know what an art director was at the time. I only found that out two years later at my second job. I asked for a pay rise and my boss said "so you want to be an art director?" and I said "yes, that's exactly what I want to be" without a clue of what it meant. I just liked the way it sounded: very glamorous. This attitude of going for things and learning as I went along has never been absent from my career. A couple of years later, when someone asked me to do an MPU (that silly square banner) I said "OK - it will be ready tomorrow", without knowing what an MPU was. So I Googled MPU, found out what it was and I spent the whole night making it.

Back to CD-ROMs: after three months of planning, me, a photographer and the project-lead (who was also the project writer) got on the newly built Eurostar, first-class, to Paris. The whole thing was like a dream: Paris, first-class AND business cards. Somehow having 500 bits of paper with my name on, misspelled of course, made me feel more proud than the bankers in 'American Psycho'.

The journey went well, the only hiccup was me being totally paranoid about the ticket inspector checking my Brazilian passport. Even though my visa was legitimate, I was afraid that my dream would end, that I would be fired and deported by a Frenchman wearing a terrible uniform, punching tickets. So I gave him not only my passport but a business card.

But the dream didn't end. It got better. We were staying at a posh hotel and I couldn't believe my luck. On the first night, I was torn between the responsibility of having to wake up at 6AM and the excitement of being in Paris getting paid for being on vacation. I knew if I thought too much I'd stay at the hotel, so I ended up putting on some jeans with my pajama top and found myself at a bar chatting to a guy as high as a Sinaloa cartel member, until 2AM. Yes I had to wake up four hours later but hey, *c'est Paris, non?*

Back in Basingstoke, we wrote this bible on how the CD-ROM was going to work and mapped out all the assets for approximately 200 screens: text, images, music and video. I volunteered to take the bible and assets to Brighton, where our developers were based. And it took us ages to save all assets on to this drive as heavy as a brick. Remember, this is the time pre-mobile phones, pre-Dropbox, there was no broadband and modems were these slow versions of faxes. We finished 15 minutes before the last train was due to depart.

On the rush to the station, the project lead hits a car in front of us. She gets out, a little dizzy and yells "Get the fuck out of the way". The other driver, a very polite Englishman, replies "But you hit me". To which she replied, "I don't care, write your number here and get the fuck out of the way". When we get to the station the train doors where closing, so I threw myself inside the train with an inch to spare of the closing doors.

I got to Brighton at 11PM with two bruises, one in my head from the crash and another on my leg from the train. I then went to see the developers who thought I was a man from speaking nerdy code with them via email (this happens quite a lot in my career) and ended up at a bar with a friend singing Pulp's "I want to live like common people" like I was some kind of rock star.

I started at my first job by doing the most complex thing I could have done from a learning curve perspective. It was like Proust skipping the short stories and going straight to 'In Search of Lost Time'. I not only had to think about how to sell what I was producing, but also put the product together doing three different jobs. After that, digital work like sites, apps etc., was easy-peasy lemon squeezy.

During this process I learned I could use the fact that I was a woman in a nerdy world to my advantage, all the way to advertising and Creative Direction status. I learned to reach for goals beyond my skills and got invariably addicted to it. I learned to love to make things, and most importantly I learned to navigate the unknown, always with a conviction that I was going to make it work.

And the combination of not knowing and really believing in something is a powerful thing. The raw fear of the uncharted combined with unconditional belief is something that can start wars, heal diseases but also, make your career.

Believing in something so much that you're willing to risk the darkness of the process with the clarity of your conviction is more valuable than all the advice in the world.

So please, don't listen to any of this if you believe you can do it.

Minna Lavola
Former Senior Creative/Partner, TBWA\Helsinki

Minna Lavola joined the company in 2002. Her path to TBWA partnership began back in 1997 at Ogilvy&Mather and continued via EuroRSCG to Leo Burnett.

She is one of the most awarded creatives in Finland with over 50 international awards, including five Cannes Lions, and numerous national prizes. She also judged at Cannes Lions.

She believes in strong visual expression and innovative media and guerilla-stunts are close to her heart.

Today Minna is starting up her own business in Helsinki.

My First Time
By Minna Lavola

Being dyslexic (worry not, my Copywriter proofread this), I never did that well in school. Luckily I was blessed with an art teacher who saw talent in my drawings and encouraged me to pursue a career in the arts. My parents were relieved: "The girl got an A in something!" and off I was to an art school in San Francisco to study Graphic Design.

I was in heaven. I had found my passion and believed everything and anything my Art Professors would tell me. Which was good, expect that one of their "wisdoms" was: "Never ever sell yourself by working in advertising. As a Graphic Designer, you can make a living while remaining "an Artist"."

After graduation I landed a job at Ogilvy Helsinki as an Art Director's assistant. I immediately announced that my title shall be changed to Graphic Designer and that I would not "do" advertising. (And ahem… no, I did not know who David Ogilvy was, bless my young arrogance). The CEO was probably thinking: "Boy, do they get self-confident in America", and let it slide.

After about a year of proudly "only Graphic Designing", luck came my way again in the form of a young copywriter, Mira Olsson, who was so passionate about advertising ideas (and who knew who David Ogilvy was), that I ended up tasting the advertising-drug, after all.

She convinced me we should team up and work on an important pitch for SAP Solutions (a Business Software provider), a high-tech and a very "un-young-girl-team –account", that seemed totally out of our reach.

We came up with a strategy and a campaign idea that we visualized with simple graphic illustrations. It did not look like a business-to-business campaign as we then knew them, and our Creative Director was hesitant.

Somehow we were able to sell it to him: "Companies do not decide, but the individuals who work for those companies do. We have to arouse their interest."

He decided to include our approach into the presentation. The Marketing Director of SAP Solutions was a woman. Perhaps he thought some young female energy would bring us goodwill amongst the male dominated competition.

Instead of the usual PowerPoint, we built a unique 3D -presentation box that folded in all directions. We created miniature landscapes to show the advertising in its real surroundings. We were so excited about the work that we forgot to be nervous.

The client was impressed. (I must admit, it felt pretty good to hear her say: "Thank goodness one agency brings me something else than that B2B bore").

"Well, CEO's and Financial Directors are people too", our Creative Director added swiftly.

We won the pitch, our client got great results and the work was nominated in a few shows. Our Creative Director told us: "Girls, enjoy the success, because you will never do anything as good as this again."

To his "disappointment" we won our first Lion for another client soon after.

What did My First Time teach me?

1. Don't let any disadvantage stop you. I later learned that Leonardo Da Vinci and Thomas Edison were also dyslexic. Wish I had known it in my school days.
2. Trust that you will get lucky against all odds, when you put in the work.

3. Don't believe everything your Art Professors (or Creative Directors) tell you.
4. Most of all, believe in yourself.

Elspeth Lynn
ECD, M&C Saatchi,London

I have been working in advertising for 22 years and consider myself very fortunate to have done so.

Over those 22 years I have worked with a number of outstanding people, have experienced much joy, and I am very proud of my career to date.

I believe that a big part of the joy in this business is not only doing work that you're proud of, but finding people that you love to work with.

Being surrounded by good and supportive people that 'have your back' can make the difference between enjoying what you do - or not.

The appreciation of others and knowing it's not just about you is key. Never underestimate how helpful a great CD, creative partner, CEO, MD, account person, planner, producer, (and in this case) a photographer and production manager can be.

Here is a story about that, and a lesson I learnt.

My First Time

By Elspeth Lynn

VIDEO:

CLIENT	TITLE	PRODUCT	JOB NUMBER
MFT	'My first Shoot'	My Career 1	
LENGTH	PAGE	VERSION	
90	1	1	

LOCATION: DDB Toronto, March 1990
SFX: Musical score underneath. Music starts with a threatening tone.

Open on a female art director in her mid-twenties. She holds a stack of contact sheets in her arms and walks hurriedly down a long corridor in an office. She appears to be upset. She goes in to a small windowless office and shuts the door behind her.

She sits down. Takes a deep breath. Her expression changes to complete sadness and tears roll down her cheek. She closes her eyes.

CUT TO MONTAGE OF FOOTAGE FROM THE PAST
SFX: Music is joyful in tone.

We see the art director walking into DDB her first day of work, she smiles at the receptionist, shakes her hand and say hello. Cut to the art director with a writer a few weeks later getting briefed by account people. We see them working late at night and there are empty fast food containers lying about. The clock reads 11:37pm. The art director is in the studio, grappling with rubber cement as she flaps about trying to mount layouts onto foamcore. We see her leaving at 2:57am.

We then see the art director and the writer earnestly presenting the work to a very mid-West American client ie conservative/flowereddress/bad hair. The client shakes her head as if to say 'no'. We see the team leave the client's office completely crushed.

We see the art director and writer working again late at night. The clock reads 2:10am.

Again the fight with the sticky rubber-backed layouts ensues until the art director looks satisfied that the campaigns are perfectly done. She rubs the side of her hand over each board. She smiles at the work.

Cut to the art director and writer meeting the client, this time at DDB. They are bursting with excitement as they hold up the layouts. The art director hauls out a photographer's book onto the table. We see the client glance at the art director and slowly nod her head in agreement.

We see the team bouncing out of the office.

We then cut to a shoot and the art director is listening to a photographer explaining the set up of the lighting. We use time lapse to see the shoot going on for 3 days. We see the sun set and rise outside the studio. The art director gets handed a loupe and she tries to use it - backwards. We see the photographer turn it right way round and they both laugh and look at the shots. They know they have it. The art director and photographer hug each other goodbye. They leave the studio. The clock reads 11:39pm.

We cut to 3 days later. The art director receives a large brown envelope. She opens it up to reveal a stack of contact sheets. She spends hours, with the loupe the right way round, staring at all the shots. She circles the ones she likes best. She proudly takes them in to show the writer. The writer looks pleased.

We then see the art director proudly walking into the Head of print Production office, who looks very grumpy and worn, in comparison to our young art director. The head of production lights up a cigarette (yes you could smoke in the office back then) and she scowls at the stack of contact sheets and looks at the art director. She blows out smoke from the side of her mouth. and nonchalantly flips though about 10 contact sheets and shakes her head.

Art Director: "What's the matter?"
Head of Production: "These shots…these shots are way too dark. They're useless-- there's nothing I can do with them. You ruined the shoot."

SFX: The music becomes very intense

We see the art director stand frozen to the floor.

Art Director: "Are you sure?"
Head of Production: "Oh yes. I'm quite sure."

We see the art director grab the contact sheets, leave the office and start to walk rapidly down the hallway.

We are now back to the present time and we see the art director sitting exactly as she was before the montage. Very upset.

She spends the next few minutes pacing in her office.

SFX: The music stops abruptly.

She picks up the phone and calls the photographer.

Photographer: "Hello?"

Art Director: "It's Elspeth (sniff sniff). The head of production has just told me that all the shots are useless … I've ruined my first shoot. I don't know what to do. Can we shoot it again? Is that model available? Oh my god… I'm beside myself"

Photographer: "What? Those shots are fine. I have no idea what she's talking about. The contact sheets are PRINTED a bit too dark but the actual FILM is perfect. The contact sheets are not what you use for production, that's just to choose the shot."

Art Director: "Ooooooohhhhhhhh. But I've just been told I screwed the whole thing up. Why would she do that?"

Photographer: "I don't know, but I can assure you 100% that the shots will be beautiful. I'm so proud of this shoot, and it was such a pleasure to work with you."

The art director wipes the tears from her eyes and breathes deeply.
She walks down back down the hall towards the Head of Production.

But she passes her office - and goes 2 doors down to see the Assistant Head of Production.

She sits down at his desk and begins to show him the shots. She explains she knows the contact sheets are too dark but the photographer has assured her the film is fine.

Assistant Head of Production: "Oh don't worry, I'll call the photographer and we'll sort it out. Let me see that shot...wow that's fantastic. We'll be fine. We just need to open up the film a bit. These will be beautiful ads...I'll help you get these done. Wow this looks like the nicest work we've ever done for this client. "

The art director smiles. She thanks him. Relieved. Tired. Pissed off, but fortunately, one bit wiser.

About photography, and how some people can be.

SFX: Music crescendos to a joyful (but not cheesy) sound.

SUPER: The only way to do great work

SUPER: Is to work with great people that help get you there.

Mónica Moro

Executive Creative Director
McCann, Madrid

Monica has spent her entire career at McCann. McCann Madrid is the only Spanish advertising agency to have made the Top 20 in the Gunn Report for several years. In Spain it was named Agency of the Year 2011, and for the third consecutive year has been the most awarded Spanish agency. Recently it has been named one of the most desirables agencies to work in.

Monica is also listed in Top Talent on The Directory Big Won Creative Rankings. Most notable are her campaigns for Coca Cola, Coca Cola Zero, or The Spanish Cancer Association, as well as her work in transforming local brands such as Campofrio and Metro of Madrid into prizewinners.

She has won over one hundred awards at the top national and international advertising festivals and her most outstanding work has been included in the collection of the Reina Sofia National Contemporary Art Museum.

Monica has served on the juries of Cannes, Clio, London, El Ojo de Iberoamérica, and El Sol festivals, among others.

She is part of the recently formed Creative Leadership Collective (CLC), an international committee from McCann Worldwide who promote and support creative excellence on the network.

She is a member of the Board of the Club de Creativos de España (CdeC, Creative Circle of Spain).

Monica holds a B.A. in Advertising and Public Relations from the Complutense University in Madrid, Spain.

My First Time
By Monica Moro

"That castaway is fat." That's what I said, but since I was on the first casting of my first shoot of my first spot, and I was only a trainee with no experience and no wage, nobody paid much attention.

But he really was too fat. Castaways are supposed to be emaciated, or at least skinny. But no matter, he got the job. My partner and I, fifteen years later, still remember how they stuck us with the fat castaway.

Against all odds, the spot with the fat castaway won a prize or two in regional festivals, which to our minds only confirmed that we were on the right track. "With a skinny castaway we would have gotten gold," we thought. What can I say; we were stubborn.

It all began a few months earlier at university. McCann had a deal for students in their final year. One of its clients would give us a real brief—in this case it was Coca-Cola, a brand which later loomed large in my career —and the prize for the best campaign would be an internship at McCann.

So our campaign won, and there we were.

We worked tirelessly for months, fuelled by stubbornness and a burning desire to learn. We memorized all the reels from Cannes and books from One Show (now there's a nice memory I had forgotten: the first book you buy because your work is in it) and bent over backwards to help the senior teams. Those were the days when they asked for one radio spot and you gave them a campaign with twenty. So much energy, so much work. So much, in fact, that many times we just slept in the agency. We would tell the doorman to call one of the offices as a wake-up call. How much fun we had.

And then one day a brief arrived for a promotion and they gave it to "the girls" (a term which stayed with us for years and which someone still uses today, which we find not only not irritating, but deeply comforting). We presented our idea about the castaway who had to be skinny, and soon after we got our first contract and first salary: 70,000 pesetas a month... about 400 euros.

The great thing about working in advertising is that you never lose that "first time" feeling. Maybe it's because it's the first time you have to sell a hybrid car and you don't even know how to drive, or the first time you come to Cannes to be on the jury or as a Young Lion, and that is the first time you sleep in a hotel room that is like a submarine capsule (I will never forget it). There is a first time when you film with Paul Arden, the first time you truly screw up in a meeting, the first time you manage teams, or the first time you create a campaign which spreads hope in a country going through a crisis, for example.
We're lucky to work at something that gives us that "first time" feeling.

And it's even better when they don't screw you with a fat castaway.

Mi Primera Vez
Por Mónica Moro

"Ese naufrago esta gordo". Eso dije, pero como era mi primer casting, del primer rodaje, de mi primer anuncio y yo solo era una trainee sin sueldo ni experiencia nadie me hizo mucho caso.

Pero el naufrago estaba súper gordo. Y los náufragos deben estar esqueléticos, o por lo menos delgados. Pero no, el gordo fue el elegido. Mi compañera y yo, quince años después, seguimos acordándonos de cómo nos colaron al gordo.

Pese a todo la película con el naufrago gordo ganó algún premio en festivales regionales, cosa que no nos hizo dudar ni un minuto de que estábamos en lo cierto. "Con uno flaco hubiera sido oro" pensamos. Y es que la cabezonería es lo nuestro.

Todo empezó unos meses antes en la facultad. McCann tenía un acuerdo para alumnos de ultimo curso. Uno de sus clientes nos daba un brief real, en este caso Coca-Cola (una marca que, por cierto, marcara mi carrera por muchos años) y la mejor campaña presentada conseguía unas practicas en la agencia.

Así que presentamos una idea que resulto ganadora, y ahí nos plantamos. Con nuestra cabezonería y mucho apasionamiento por aprender estuvimos varios meses trabajando a lo bestia. Desde estudiar de memoria todas las bobinas de Cannes y aprenderte los libros del One Show (bonito recuerdo que había olvidado: el primer libro que te compras porque aparece tu trabajo en él) a ayudar en todo lo q podias a los equipos seniors. Esa época en la que te pedían una cuña de radio y presentabas una campaña de veinte. Cuanta energía. Cuanto trabajo. Tanto, que varios días optábamos por quedarnos a dormir en la agencia. Avisábamos al portero del edificio de que nos llamara al teléfono de uno de los despachos a modo de wake up call. Y cuanto nos divertimos.

Y en una de estas, llego un brief de una promoción y nos lo dieron a "las niñas" (por cierto, ese apelativo nos acompañó durante muchos años y todavía hoy alguien lo sigue usando, algo que más que molestar resulta absolutamente tranquilizador). Presentamos la idea del naufrago que tenía que ser flaco, y al poco tiempo llegó un primer contrato y un primer sueldo: 70000 pesetas al mes, unos 400 euros.

Lo bueno de trabajar en publicidad es que uno no para de experimentar esa sensación de lo que significa "la primera vez". Puede que sea porque por primera vez tengas que vender un coche con motor híbrido y ni siquiera sabes conducir, o por que es la primera vez que vas a Cannes como jurado o lo haces como young lion y duermes por primera vez en un hotel que parece la cápsula de un submarino (no lo olvidare). Hay una primera vez para filmar con Paul Arden, una primera vez para cagarla en una reunión, una primera vez para manejar equipos o una primera vez para hacer una campaña que contagie de optimismo a un país en crisis, por ejemplo.
Somos afortunados por trabajar en algo que provoca una sensación de estreno casi a diario.

Eso sí, que nadie te la joda con un naufrago gordo.

Mira Olsson
Founder/Creative Director
Lovely, Amsterdam

Mira Olsson is co-founder of Lovely, an advertising agency based in Amsterdam.

During her years at Ogilvy, TBWA and Bob Helsinki, she became one of the most internationally acclaimed advertising creatives in Finland with numerous Cannes Lions, New York Festivals, Eurobest and Epica awards.

Before settling in Amsterdam she also enjoyed working with people she admires in advertising agencies in Cape Town, London and Los Angeles.

My First Time
By Mira Olsson

It was the early nineties. I was fresh out of Business School and had gotten a job in marketing with a decent salary, a company car and a company (mobile!) phone. I had made it, shoulder pads and all.

In came a phone call. As a late reply to one of the job applications I had sent a half a year earlier, the CEO of the hottest ad agency in Finland would give me fifteen minutes of his time to tell me about the field (yes, I'd call it a miracle too). In the coolest office I've ever seen, he gave me a fascinating presentation about "How it's smarter for a brand to not be liked by everyone, but to be liked A LOT by a certain group of people, who would then be loyal to it."

I must have nodded in the right moments of his monologue, because while walking me out he mentioned that their receptionist was going on maternity leave and that perhaps I'd be interested in filling in for her for the next six months: "Think about it and call my secretary tomorrow if you want the job."

A dilemma: Shall I keep the "dream job" with benefits, which fit my degree and all my friends envied? Or switch it to a six-month low-pay stint answering the phone and making coffee? To add to the dilemma, Finland was in its deepest depression since the Second World War. If I took the stint, there was no guarantee for ANY job for me when it was over.

For no logical reason whatsoever I resigned and accepted the offer the next morning.

It turned out the reception was the perfect place to observe what an interesting and inspiring field it was. My mom was seemingly disappointed when I came home convinced that one day I was going to be a Copywriter. "What is that? You sure you wouldn't rather aim for Account Manager?"

166

During the evenings I'd stay in late and admire the work in all the old award books and during the days I'd eavesdrop in meetings to learn as much as I could.

Then came my lucky break. A Copywriter was working on a Volvo Campaign. The press campaign needed a third headline. The presentation was tomorrow. I memorized the other two headlines, casually asked for some background info of the goals and target group of the campaign and went home to think. Then it came, like a lightning around midnight.

The line.

It did not feel as if I had come up with it, it was more as if it was sent "from above". Even I, with my nonexistent experience, knew it was a good one.

The next morning I nervously waited for the Copywriter to show up. I approached him with extreme caution (I had been in an advertising agency long enough to know that
    1. He had not cracked it yet, and
    2. Disturbing a creative two hours before a presentation he has not cracked yet is not a good idea and shared "The line" with him.

He loved it. The client loved it. Cannes loved it.

But my six-month contract was over. The company could not give me job, because of their "no-juniors policy" (which, to be fair, they changed a few years later). But I was hooked." Then, because of "the line" and a couple of scribbled visual ideas in my portfolio, I finally (sixteen rejections and an excruciatingly long year later) got a job as a Junior Copywriter at a smaller agency. My Copywriting career had started.

A few things I've learned along the way:

1. Study what's been done. Look at all the past work you can get your hands on. Since Bill Bernbach. Not only will you be very inspired and impressed, you'll also learn the basic craft of Ideas.

2. It's hard to get in. If you want it enough, you will eventually, but you'll probably have to settle for very low pay in the beginning. Never give up. It only takes one piece of great work and you're in for good and proper pay follows.

3. Don't hide your ideas. Share them all. Even, if someone else takes credit for them. The more you share them the more ideas you'll keep having.

4. Be happy for the great work of your colleagues. (Sounds easy, but I've seen many creatives suffering year after year from other people's successes. What a waste!) Someone put it wisely: "Success does not bring happiness. Happiness brings success."

5. Listen to your gut feeling.

6. Be ruthless with your work. You know when an idea IS great (OR when you're trying to explain something into a great idea, when you're exhausted working on it). When you finally get The Idea, all the pain will be worth it.

Karin Onsager-Birch
Executive Creative Director
Ogilvy / Blue Hive, London

Karin recently moved back to Europe to take the helm as ECD at The Blue Hive in London. Her current responsibility is to guide and mentor the creative on Ford across all media and across the continent.

Half Norwegian, half Mexican, Karin grew up in Norway and studied design in Switzerland. After getting degrees in Advertising and Graphic Design from the Art Center Pasadena, Karin spent most of her career at Goodby, Silverstein & Partners, in San Francisco, AdAge's 'Agency of the Decade.'

During her tenure there, she worked on accounts that creative people dream about—Nike, Porsche, Adobe, Haagen-Dazs, Hyundai and Kayak.com. Her work has garnered honors from Cannes, Clios, The One Show, The Library of Congress and she is also a frequent award show judge and speaker.

She counts herself extremely lucky to get to travel the world doing something she loves. Collaborating with talented and interesting people, creating exciting ideas, making beautiful, funny and smart work.

Karin's energy and passion for the business is infectious. To quote Jeff Goodby: "Her smile enters a room before she does, and she brings an energy to things that inspires juniors, clients, account people and me."

My First Time
By Karin Onsager-Birch

"$90 a day, with no benefits?" I exclaimed, anguished. This was a puny salary, even for a junior AD like me, just out of school.

"Yeah, but you'll get credit on anything you work on here at "The Dynamite Lab" (names have been changed to fake civility and protection.) "Which counts for a lot more than going to any of those hack agencies who are making you offers", said the famous writer/creative director who shall remain nameless, as he swung a baseball bat around the tiny room of his upstart agency. The place had been getting a bit of notice in the ad press as a new hip boutique to watch. All my friends were jealous of me having landed a job there.

After two weeks of odd projects like blowing up naked shots of my boss's newly buff chest, making posters out of them to send to a girl he was courting, and wrapping Tiffany boxes for her, the nameless asshole hands me a paragraph on a piece of paper and says: "Here, turn this script into a spot. It's for Rhino Records, and it's gonna run on MTV."

It was a very simple idea, it could work in a single shot, I thought. "We're staring at the back of a man walking down a desert road, " he said. "He comes to a dry cowpie in the middle of the road. He kicks it out of the road and keeps walking. At this point, loud music kicks in. SUPER: MTV120 Minutes Compilation. "NO MIDDLE OF THE ROAD SHIT." I was incredibly excited.

My boss went out of town and I wasted no time writing up some visual directions and creating a storyboard. I invited a friend over and put him in boots, grabbed the Polaroid camera and put him in the middle of our street. I took photos of every possible angle, then traced them into a desert landscape and added the title and product shot of the CD cover to the storyboard. Then I came up with 10-12 print ad just in case they'd want more around the idea.

My boss, "Missing in Action Asshole," called and said that he needed me to head down to Rhino Records headquarters to present and sell the commercial. My first client meeting ever! And for a TV project! And all by myself!

Nervous, I dressed up and went to the client, presented the idea as best I could and sold it. Rhino was very pleased—a good idea and cheap to make.

I couldn't wait for the day of the shoot. I drove to the desert with a very nice and experienced freelance producer from Seattle. At a desolate desert road (our little set on it) I met Kinka Usher, a young DP who was trying to break into directing. He was willing to do it for the opportunity and the director credit (very little money). We hit it off immediately and discussed angles and shots. All that cool shoot shit. I thought I'd died and gone to heaven.

My boss had cast himself as the talent (enough said) and was wearing a very tight T-shirt to proudly show off his newly buff bod. We had lots of extra dry cowpies on hand, so Kinka was able to get several takes on tracks and a few hand held with a Bolex. Great coverage on a simple, inexpensive little idea. The spot was edited quickly and turned out fun and a little edgy. My boss entered it into award shows. My first TV spot!

Clock-wipe: 2 months later I'm at the Beldings, the LA Awards show, on the arm of my boyfriend. Chiat/Day is sweeping the show. Lots of great stuff. Energizer Bunny "Dances with your feet" wins best 30 sec commercial. Then comes the category for spots produced for under $10K. (This is the under $100K category now, I think.)

They show the Bronze and Silver winners. Then—drum-roll—"Gold goes to The Dynamite Lab for Rhino Records: No middle of the road shit!" I jumped up and down, elated. All these fancy Creative Directors from the LA Ad Community, who held my future in their hands, were gonna see my name in the credits!

My pulse was racing as they flashed them. And there they stood in big letters on the screen:

Creative Director	HUGE ASSHOLE
Copywriter	HUGE ASSHOLE
Art Director	HUGE ASSHOLE
Film Director	HUGE ASSHOLE

Stacked above itself 4 times in all cap letters, my boss's name.

Kinka Usher called me furious the next day, he had heard what had happened to both of us and was outraged. The show was on a Saturday night. Monday I didn't go to work— Tuesday either. When the office manager called on Wednesday to ask where I was, I told her to have El ASSHOLE GIGANTE call me and apologize. Needless to say, he never called. And I never went back.

I learned that being talented or famous or getting a lot of good press doesn't stop anyone from being a thief, a coward or both.

I was offered my dream job at job at Goodby, Silverstein & Partners a few months later. Kinka signed as a director with a production company and became very in demand. The "Dynamite Lab" enjoyed some success employing and exploiting other students, paying them almost nothing, and then fizzled out.

I don't think Asshole Boss ever got that girl. Karma maybe.

Liz Paradise
EVP, Group Creative Director
McKinney

Though a northerner by birth, Liz has spent her advertising career in the warmth and humidity of the South. Except for four years as a copywriter at The Martin Agency, she has devoted her talent and passion for great work to McKinney. Liz became a GCD in the late '90s and has touched the vast majority of brands to come through the agency. She has created some of the agency's most memorable and award-winning work.

Her accolades include awards from The One Show, The One Show Interactive, Communication Arts, D&AD, Cannes, the MIXX Awards and Art Directors Club. Currently, Liz directs McKinney's work on Nationwide, GNC and Mizuno.

In the past she's written for and overseen Audi, Nasdaq, Aetna, Polaris Industries, Lands' End, Virgin Atlantic Airways and Select Comfort. Liz is a graduate of The University of North Carolina at Chapel Hill.

My First Time
By Liz Paradise

Back in the day, there was a medium called print. It was a beautiful medium in so many ways. At its best, it was wonderfully simple – no moving parts, things to click on or mobile versions to create. It was highly visual – in a clean, without 30 branding elements, kind of way. And it was also the place where writers could really write – provocative headlines and long copy could win you pencils.

My first portfolio was nearly 75% print, so suffice to say my apparent ability in it was what got me hired at McKinney. McKinney being the first agency to win the Kelly Award for print.

Now cut to my first day at work. My first assignment. I couldn't have been more excited – a magazine ad for a cruise line. What a golden opportunity to show my stuff. Until I realized it was for a 1/8 page ad. Text only.

What followed were 5 of the most angst filled hours of my career. Seriously – how could I be writing about it this many years later (and I do mean many years) unless it was painfully etched in my mind?

Regardless of having no space whatsoever, I couldn't just write something straightforward. Not for my first assignment. I HAD to find a way to turn it into a creative miracle.

I tried and I tried and I tried, but every time I figured out how to give it any personality, it was at the cost of including the mandatory content. You know, like the name of the company and phone number.

I pulled out a lot of hair. Perspired rather heavily. And truth be told, had a few tears in my eyes. Eventually I had to go present to my CD, who was, and still is, one of the most writerly writers I know.

I sheepishly handed her what I had typed. I think "Call to book your vacation" was the most creative part of it. She studied it carefully with quite a serious look on her face. I was pretty sure she hated it and me.

And then it came.

She put it down on her desk. Broke out in a huge smile and said, "Very nice, Liz. You've passed the first test. Know when there's creative opportunity and when it's more important to tell it straight."

It wasn't fun at the time, but to this day, I use that lesson. As much as we'd like to, we can't lay a golden egg every time. Some days it simply is okay to get it done and not get in the way of ourselves. It really is okay.

Marlena Peleo-Lazar
Chief Creative Officer
Vice President
McDonald's USA

Marlena Peleo-Lazar was born and raised in Detroit. (Yes, she does know all of the lyrics to all of the Motown songs.) After receiving degrees in English and Media Studies, she set her sights on becoming the next Barbara Walters in television. On her way to "stardom" she was recruited by Leo Burnett to be a copywriter. And, it is there she spent her formative years, rising through the creative ranks to become a global creative director on such notable Brands as Procter & Gamble and Kellogg's. In 1997, she clicked the heels of her ruby slippers and became the creative leader of Ogilvy & Mather/Chicago working on such accounts as Sears, Kimberly Clark, Illinois Lottery, and Unilever. Marlena has a history of Brand building and creating award-winning creative.

Today, Marlena is the Chief Creative Officer/Vice President of McDonald's Corporation where she is responsible for all of the advertising for Brand McDonald's. She was instrumental in the creation and implementation of the current business-building, creative, award-winning "i'm lovin' it" advertising campaign for McDonald's. In 2004, her career and efforts on behalf of McDonald's were honored with the Chicago Advertising Woman of the Year Award. Subsequent to this, Marlena also received the Illinois Influential Women in Business Award, the McDonald's Women's Leadership Network Award, and a host of industry creative awards.

When not helping to polish the "golden arches," Marlena is active in the Chicago advertising community. In 2006 and 2007, she served as President of the Chicago Advertising Federation. She is often a featured speaker at industry events and at schools throughout the country. Additionally, Marlena mentors many people seeking careers in advertising and marketing.

Marlena is married to John Lazar and is kept "forever young" by her two sons, Christopher and Brendan.

Current Board Participation: Girl Scouts of America
                                 Chicago Advertising Federation

My First Time
By Marlena Peleo-Lazar

First, we need to set the record straight. My first ad was not created on the side of a cave. In fact, there was electricity. And, yes, television had been invented. But, OK, it did happen a while ago. We actually have proof of this momentous event. There I am in a photo, big, permed hair. Cool "creative" outfit (or what I thought was supposed to be cool). Arm draped on the director's shoulder. Big smile. Oh wait, freezing to death. It's like 10 degrees. Not warm, sunny, L.A. Really cold Flemington, New Jersey. But even remembering this long ago moment, I know that I was breathless. Not just from the cold. It is my first "big-time" commercial shoot.

I hope that I am not cheating when I count this as my first one. Until this point, my career in advertising largely consisted of writing the middle announcer sections for spots. "This week, large jumbo eggs, AND Kleenex tissue are all on sale. And don't forget to have some summer fun! Starkist Tuna just..." After a brief stay at a Detroit ad agency that specialized in retail advertising, I was hired out of school to work at Leo Burnett. I would like to say that this was always my career ambition, since I spent many happy productive years there. No, I actually aspired to being something like Meryl Streep. (If that didn't work out, I figured I could slide into Barbara Walters' career and interview people like Anwar Sadat or Liz Taylor). When you are 21 years old, you usually don't think long-term goals. At least I sure didn't. My plan was to try advertising for six months, then achieve "stardom" somewhere else.

I interviewed at Leo Burnett on a Thursday and began work on the following Monday. This was no small feat considering that I didn't even live in Chicago, but Detroit. But they were generous enough to put me up in a hotel for a couple of weeks until I could land an apartment to live in.

Unlike, I am sure, many people starting out today who are smart enough to ask stuff like, "What will I be working on?" Or "Who will I be working with?" I wasn't. I was just proud to be working at the legendary Leo Burnett. The home of the Marlboro Man! Flying the Friendly Skies! Charlie the Tuna!

I however, wasn't assigned to any of those accounts. Instead, I was to start right away on Cheer detergent or "All-Tempa" Cheer as it was coined. Unlike the mighty Tide, Cheer kept your bright colored clothes extra bright because you washed them in cold water. OK, got it!

But apparently, I didn't. I wrote one script after another to no avail. I happened to work for a creative director who was as demanding as they come. My scripts weren't "fun" enough. Then, they were too funny. The "logic flow" was off. The scripts are too logical. I felt like Goldilocks and the Three Bears. Worse, a failure before I even really began a career.

When I was relegated to packing the black bag for client meetings – do they even have such a thing anymore? – was when I was certain that this wasn't the job for me. It was not until much later that I was told that, in fact, this was a BIG HONOR. While you were not invited to attend, let alone to present, in any important meeting, only the most promising young copywriters got to do this task. (I owe my superior spray mount skills to putting tabs on boards).

As you can imagine, by the time I actually got approval from the creative director, I was jumping for joy. (I now think that under that crabby exterior there was a heart – albeit a black one).

Nonetheless, we were off...to the client. We will skip over the gory details of the countless revisions. It might read too much like the gym scene in the movie _Carrie_. All that really mattered was that I WAS GOING OUT ON PRODUCTION! So what that the spot was supposed to take place in the summer, not in the dead of winter? Who cared that we couldn't afford to go to California? The New York area, we hear, is quite balmy in December! At least the director would be the famous Bob Giraldi.

Now, landing him to do this commercial was in no small thanks to the wonderful producer, Angelo Antonucci, who we know to this day must have promised Giraldi/Suarez Company all future jobs from LBC just to do this. As much as I loved my art, it was no Lee Clow *1984*. It was just a story of a woman remembering her class trip where she decked herself out in her best white outfit to travel.

The story begins in black and white then switches to present day color where she lets you know that the world has changed to brighter colors. That's why, my friends, you need All-Tempa Cheer!

OK. It wasn't Chekhov. In fact, it might have run only about five times on TV because the client decided to change the strategy for the brand. It was enough, however, for my family to see it. Best of all, it got me promoted out of having to pack the black bag for meetings.

So many years ago…so many lessons learned.

A few –
- *No job is ever too small.*

We actually had to go to a Laundromat a day before the shoot and wash the clothes to fulfill the legal requirements. To this day, "my whites are whiter, my colors bright."
- *I learned early on that sometimes you've got to be creative about being creative.*

If L.A. is not in the cards, make New York amazing.
- *"Write It Better"*

That's what my first creative director gave as direction. He might have been a challenge, but I now get it. Good is never good enough. Be relentless in achieving creative excellence in everything.
- *Wear A Heavy Coat And Comfortable Shoes.*

183

You seem to always freeze on shoots – especially if it's an early morning shoot in L.A. It's good advice for a career and life, too.

- *Your one-millionth shoot, your job should be as wonderful as your first.*

Enough said.

Anna Qvennerstedt
Creative Director, Senior Partner and Chairman
Forsman & Bodenfors, Stockholm

Anna Qvennerstedt is a Creative Director, Senior Partner and Chairman of Forsman & Bodenfors in Stockholm, Sweden. Before joining the agency in 2004 she was a founding partner at TBWA Stockholm.

In 2007, Anna was awarded the Platinum Egg as the youngest person ever given this prize honoring individuals who have had an exceptional impact on the advertising industry in Sweden. She has also twice received the Swedish copywriting award and won numerous national and international awards, including a Grand Prix in Cannes.

Anna has served as a juror on several award shows, such as the Cannes Lions, Eurobest, D&AD and the One Show. In 2011 she was named Jury President of the Swedish national ad awards (as the first woman ever).

My First Time
By Anna Qvennerstedt

I won my very first award in advertising school, after finishing the first term. I wasn't aware that there were going to be any prizes and I was immensely proud. My knees were shaking when I went up in front of everybody to collect it. I remember thinking that this – this is the only award I will ever win.

The prize consisted of a marzipan pig. The front was dipped in chocolate and it had silvery eyes. A red ribbon was tied around it. I brought my trophy home and put it on a shelf. I don't know how long it took me, maybe a week? What can I say, I love sweets and my fridge was probably empty. So I took a big bite, I ate the head with eyes and everything and then I lay awake for hours in a state of anxiety. I had eaten the only award I would ever win, at least half of it. The buttocks still stood proudly on the shelf to remind me.

To this day I find it curious that someone as insecure as myself has managed to make it in the advertising business.

I remember writing my first campaign as a copywriter. I teamed up with a senior art director in order to create a small campaign for a Finnish glass designer. Just a poster, a brochure and a few small print ads. The client was charismatic, arrogant and 20 years older than me. I was in meetings with him regularly but he wouldn't speak to me – only to the art director who was more experienced. (And male.)

Every meeting left me feeling like a nobody. Bullied, almost. All my confidence was lost in a second. I would vividly imagine myself being fired, declared an idiot, doomed to go back to the McDonald's fryer that I came from.

But when we were through with the poster and the print ads, it turned out that the copy played a major part. In fact, there were no pictures at all. Just the text I wrote.

And by the time the campaign was released, I finally got recognition from the client. If I remember correctly, he almost apologised for not believing in me. It was a small campaign, but it brought the agency its first award.

I guess that however insecure and stupid I felt in meetings, I had somehow managed to believe in myself when it came to writing. When it was just the computer and me, I could delete his influence.

It is still my best trick when it comes to writing. When I have a messy brief, a complicated client, when lots of people of different opinions try to influence the process – I try to write as if it was only me, writing to someone I respect.

It may sound easy but it's not. I have worked in advertising for almost 20 years, and I still feel insecure a lot of the time. But what I have learnt over the years is that I *appear* confident.

I think I first realised it when I was interviewed on TV, some twelve or fifteen years ago. I felt totally lost at that moment. A sweet and talkative make up-artist had given me way too heavy make-up and huge hair that made me feel extra stupid. (I didn't have the guts to tell her to take it down a bit.) The interview took over 30 minutes and it was hot in the studio and I could feel my gaze wandering and sweat running as I was stumbling on the answers. This was a recorded TV-show and it took a few weeks before it aired on TV. During that time, I panicked. I wanted to flee the country. It was just a matter of weeks, days, hours until I would be the laughingstock of the nation.

So the day came. With a hammering heart I sat down to look at the show. And to my great surprise, *I appeared totally calm*. I did stumble once or twice, but so does everyone. Overall I seemed collected and well-reasoned with slightly big hair.

Who would have thought?

That experience together with a few more of the same sort has taught me that what's going on inside and what the world around me perceive, are totally different things. That is very comforting. I think it's called experience.

My conclusion is that however tough, demanding and fault-finding this business is, you don't have to be self-confident to succeed in it.

In fact, insecurity is a good place to start. Insecurity will make you listen. Insecurity will make you sharper. Insecurity will make the whole thing feel important, like your job is on the line, and you will have to look inside yourself to find something you can honestly believe in.

This is what my career has been about so far. I stick my head out and fear that someone is going to behead me. Sometimes they do. In fact, they just did. But a few weeks after this last experience I can safely say that I can't do this in any other way. I can't do it half hearted. I can't treat it like it's "only advertising". To me, this is an extremely important job and I feel shaky a lot of the time. That hasn't changed since I was a student.

And were I to win another marzipan pig, I would probably eat it.

Min Första Tid
Av Anna Qvennerstedt

Jag vann mitt första pris när jag gick på Berghs, vid julavslutningen efter första terminen. Jag hade ingen aning om att det skulle delas ut några priser och jag blev oerhört glad att jag vann. Jag kände mig darrig när jag gick upp och hämtade priset. Och jag minns att jag tänkte att det här – det här är det enda pris jag någonsin kommer att vinna.

Priset bestod av en marsipangris. Framdelen var doppad i choklad och den hade silverkulor som ögon. Ett rött sidenband var knutet runt magen. Jag tog hem grisen och ställde den på en hylla. Sen vet jag inte exakt hur lång tid det tog, kanske en vecka? Jag har inget att säga till mitt försvar, jag är löjligt svag för sötsaker och kunde inte låta bli helt enkelt. Jag bet huvudet av grisen med ögon och allt, och sedan låg jag och ojade mig i timmar innan jag kunde somna. Jag hade ätit det enda reklampris jag någonsin skulle vinna. Åtminstone hälften av det. Bakdelen stod fortfarande kvar på hyllan med sitt sidensnöre.

Än idag finner jag det märkvärdigt att någon som är så osäker som jag kan göra karriär i reklambranschen.

Jag minns när jag skulle skriva min första egentliga kampanj som copywriter. Jag jobbade ihop med en mer erfaren art director och vi skulle göra en liten aktivitet för finska iittala. En affisch, en broschyr och några printannonser i små format. Uppdragsgivaren var en karismatisk och auktoritär man som var drygt 20 år äldre än jag. Jag träffade honom upprepade gånger i möten, men han pratade aldrig direkt med mig. Bara med art directorn. Som ju var mer erfaren. Och man.

För varje nytt möte kände jag mig allt dummare. Mobbad, nästan. Allt självförtroende rann av mig. Jag kunde livligt föreställa mig hur jag skulle få sparken, bli allmänt idiotförklarad och tvingas tillbaka till fritösen på Mc Donald's där jag inledde mitt yrkesliv.

Men när vi var klara med affischen och annonserna visade det sig att copytexten fick en framskjuten roll. Kampanjen innehöll inga bilder alls. Bara texten som jag skrivit. Och så småningom fick jag faktiskt något slags erkännande av uppdragsgivaren. Jag vill minnas att han halvt om halvt bad om ursäkt för att han inte hade trott på mig. Så småningom fick vi ett silverägg (byråns första) för kampanjen.

Jag hade känt mig dum och osäker i möten, men på något sätt hade jag väl lyckats återupprätta självkänslan när jag skulle skriva. När det var datorn och jag.

Det är fortfarande mitt bästa trick när det gäller skrivande. När briefen är otydlig, när kunden är rörig, när det finns en massa olika åsikter som man inte vet hur man ska navigera i – då gäller det att hitta till det där läget där man skriver helt utifrån sig själv, lika okomplicerat som om man skrev till en vettig människa i sin bekantskapskrets.

Det låter kanske enkelt, men det är det ju inte. Jag har jobbat med reklam i nästan 20 år, och jag känner mig fortfarande osäker rätt ofta. Men med åren har jag insett att det inte märks. Att jag framstår som betydligt säkrare än vad jag är.

Jag förstod det första gången när jag skulle intervjuas i TV. Det måste vara 12-15 år sedan. Jag kände mig som en komplett idiot där och då. Det började redan i sminket. Jag fick en alldeles för kraftig make up och ett stort hår som jag kände mig dum i. Men jag hade inte riktigt modet att be den rara make up-artisten dämpa det hela, och sen fortsatte det lika illa. Intervjun tog 30 minuter och det var kokhett i studion. Jag kände hur jag flackade med blicken och hur svetten rann medan jag snubblade på orden. TV-programmet skulle sändas först några veckor efter inspelningen, och under den tiden kände jag mig panikslagen. Jag ville fly landet. Om bara några veckor, dagar och timmar skulle jag vara rikspucko i TV på bästa sändningstid.

Så var det dags. Med galopperande hjärta slog jag mig ner för att se eländet. Men till min stora förvåning gav jag ett alldeles lugnt intryck i TV. Jag snubblade väl på ett eller annat ord, men det gör ju alla. På det stora hela framstod jag som en samlad och genomtänkt person med stort hår. Vem kunde ha anat?

Den upplevelsen, och några liknande, har lärt mig att vad som pågår inombords och vad som uppfattas av omvärlden är två helt olika saker. Det är betryggande. Jag tror att det kallas för erfarenhet.

Min slutsats är följande: Den här branschen är tuff och krävande, men man behöver inte vara självsäker för att lyckas i den.

Tvärtom tror jag att osäkerhet är en bra början. Osäkerhet gör dig ödmjuk för uppgiften. Osäkerhet gör att du skärper dig. Om du är osäker tar du alltihop på allvar och nöjer dig inte förrän du hittar en väg som du tror på.

Det är vad min karriär har handlat om hittills. Jag sticker ut huvudet så att det känns obehagligt och väntar på att någon ska halshugga mig. Ibland gör någon det. Det hände till exempel för bara några veckor sedan.

Men det är enda sättet. Jag kan inte göra det halvhjärtat. Förhållningssättet "det är ju bara reklam" har aldrig funkat för mig. Jag tycker att jag har ett enormt viktigt jobb och jag känner mig skakis ganska ofta. Det har inte ändrats sedan jag var reklamstudent.

Och om jag skulle råka vinna ännu en marsipangris, så skulle jag nog äta upp den också.

Tiffany Rolfe
Partner/Chief Content Officer
CoCollective

Tiffany Rolfe recently joined Co as Partner/Chief Content Officer from Crispin Porter + Bogusky where she was the VP/Executive Creative Director of the CP+B LA office and oversaw Old Navy and Microsoft among others.

During her ten years at CP+B, Tiffany pushed to create business-changing work for all her clients. Her client list includes American Express OPEN, MINI Cooper, Volkswagen, Microsoft, Ikea, Burger King, Virgin Atlantic Airlines, Kraft, Bolthouse Farms, and Old Navy.

While running American Express OPEN, she was responsible for the naming and launch of the Plum Card, as well as creating the successful online small business community, OPEN Forum. She worked on the 'truth' brand, which proved to be one of the most successful campaigns to curb teen smoking. Most recently, her "Eat 'em like Junk food" work for Bolthouse Farms rebranded carrots in the battle against junk food and became a highly visible campaign in the ongoing debate about health and obesity.

Tiffany's work has been featured on the cover of the New York Times, in the Wall Street Journal, Huffington Post, AdAge, Adweek, Salon, and many others. She has received top awards at every major creative and effectiveness competitions in the industry, including The One Show, D&AD, The Clios, The Andys, The Effies, and Cannes, where her work was awarded a Grand Prix and Titanium Lion. Tiffany was featured in AdAge's "Twenty Five Twenty-Somethings," in Adweek's "Young Ones," and in 2009 as one of AdAge's "Women to Watch."

My First Time
By Tiffany Rolfe

There were a few firsts I experienced on my first shoot. It was my first infommercial. My first trip to the favelas of Rio. My first meal of Pao de Queijos (Brazilian cheese puffs) from a street cart. And then my first encounter with an evil stomach parasite.

But first, I had just began my career at Crispin Porter + Bogusky as an Art Director. The agency was smaller then, just around 115 people. In the creative department, there were really no Creative Director titles. Everyone was just an Art Director or a Writer. I didn't realize at the time how great this was for a junior Art Director coming in. It meant great ideas won, not seniority.

Through my tireless work and late nights, I quickly earned a reputation as being a hard worker, perhaps even a little insane. I wanted to make as much as possible. So you could usually find me at all hours at my desk wrapped in a CPB blanket. The Miami heat ensured that every building was air-conditioned to a cool 30 degrees. I never wore more sweaters than when I lived in Miami. Instead of a hot little bikini, my uniform was wool CPB Schwag.

Because I was always at the office, it also meant that I would work with any writers who didn't have a partner at the time. I was a bit of a creative swinger. I had my regular daytime partner, and then I would moonlight with whomever else needed a partner at night. Which happened to very talented writers like Franklin Tipton and Rob Reilly.

Our clients were much smaller than the ones we have at the 1200 person CP+B office of today. Getting to make TV was rare. I had been fortunate enough to sell a couple of spots already, but didn't get to go on the shoots. We didn't normally do TV for MINI since their budgets were small. But we had an idea to do Direct Response TV, since it was affordable. Yes, an infomercial.

The integrated campaign we sold for this infomercial was called MINI Counterfeits. Since MINIs had an iconic look, with the bulldog stance, bonnet strips and contrasting roof color, they idea was that they were being counterfeited like Rolexes. Crappy big and small cars were trying to pretend they were MINIS by painting on bonnet stripes, and using oversized MINI logos to make the car look smaller. So we were going to warn the public of what to watch for.

However, we discovered that if you do an infomercial you have to sell something. So we created an informative DVD and kit to warn and help the public spot counterfeit MINIS. There were also fake ads in AutoTrader magazines, a dealer brochure, the official Counter-Counterfeit Committee website, and fake counterfeit car appearances. Since our budget was so small, the production company decided to produce the videos in Rio. And so that meant to get everything done on budget and on time, we needed to shoot everything there.

We arrived in Rio. It was sunny and beautiful and there were a good number of Giselle Bundgens' milling about. We were staying in an exotic and famously named place the Copacabana, but it was no boondoggle. We had an intense schedule of building all the counterfeit cars and then shooting all the print, video and web assets over the next 3 weeks.

Building the cars meant that we were scouring junkyards in Brazil looking for old metal car parts and junk that could pass for counterfeit MINI parts. Which also meant that there was no tasty catering trucks and craft service tables. We were eating near the rural junkyards. All seemed to be going fine, and then on about the sixth day of prep I sampled a local snack, a cheesy bread ball called Pao de Queijo. They were delicious and I ate about 6 of them. 6 too many.

That night, and for the next 2 weeks, my insides were a disaster. I'll save you from the gory details, but I couldn't eat or drink without revisiting it a few seconds later. I wouldn't stop working though. As I mentioned, I'm a bit insane. I kept fighting through it and ate the Brazilian equivalent to Pepto Bismol and Advil. Let me tell you, it wasn't very fun shooting in the middle of a village without plumbing.

Finally, after a long hot day of shooting, even blowing up a car, I walked into my hotel room and just dropped down on my bed, shoes on, still holding my computer. And didn't wake up for about 24 hours. When I finally woke, I freaked out because I'd missed some of the shoot and called Andrew Keller. He told me I was fired if I showed up at the shoot. So I rested and regained my strength, and still visited the bathroom frequently.

I finished out the rest of the shoot much weaker and 10 pounds thinner, but got everything done. I was proud of the work we did. While I never do work to try to win awards, it ended up winning the Titanium Lion, the first official year of the Titaniums, among others, as well as selling a ton of MINIS. It was worth it.

This experience taught me some of my first and most lasting lessons: Don't be afraid of small budgets and seemingly bad assignments like infomercials. When you start out, work hard and sometimes late because the best stuff can happen at night and when you are uncomfortably cold. And don't eat cheeseballs from Brazilian street vendors. Packaged foods in mini bars are totally worth the extra cost. Unless you need to shed a few extra pounds before bikini season.

Gabriella Scardaccione
Founding Parner, Executive Creative Director
Madre, Buenos Aires

Gabriela Scardaccione is a Founding Partner of Madre, the Mother office in Latin America.

She's been recently chosen as one of the fifty most influential businesswomen in Argentina, and her agency has just won the Grand Prix for best TV Campaign at the Creative Circle in Argentina, Grand Prix at APG for best planning campaign with Banco Hipotecario and Agency of the year at APG for best performance with multi-brand managing. Lucchetti, one of the main brands that her agency manages, is the most popular ad campaign with one and a half million fans in Facebook (a phenomenal achievement, for a population of forty million in Argentina). With Gabriela heading Madre, the agency was chosen by industry vote as Agency of the Year in 2010. Agency awards include Cannes Lions, Grand Prix in El Ojo de Iberoamerica, El Sol de San Sebastian and FIAP.

Gabriela started her career in Buenos Aires and then moved to London together with her husband and partner Carlos Bayala. She worked in Mother London as an Art Director for two years before moving to

StrawberryFrog in Amsterdam. Her studies include Saint Martins College of Art and Design and London College of Printing. Together with Carlos she does not only share Madre, but a beautiful son called Domingo.

My First Time
By Gabriela Scardaccione

I began my career in Buenos Aires back in the 90's and, for about six years, worked in several agencies. After a while I met my husband, Carlos, at a creative festival. We were in our late twenties and our careers were quite consolidated, but we were bored. We thought: "If someone is watching a movie about our lives, they're probably falling asleep by now".

We both worked as creatives in very good agencies in Buenos Aires, but felt the need for a bigger challenge. So sure, we could have bought a big house and settled, but we decided to spend all our savings in what it would later be the trip that would change our lives. So we got married and decided to go for a long honeymoon in London.

As an Art Director, I've always wanted to find the time to get into drawing, photography, typography and painting schools, so for two years that's what I did. I enrolled at Central Saint Martins and The London College of Printing and went back to being a student at the age of 30. It felt very refreshing. My husband went even further and got his Master's degree in Fine Art Media at the Slade School of Arts (UCL). He graduated with Honors (I have to mention this because it makes me too proud!).

Time was slipping through our fingers and so were our savings (London is a very expensive city, especially if you come with pesos from South America). We loved the life in Europe but eventually we came to realize the only way we could stay was by getting a job.

And here comes the story of my second first time.

We had never worked together before. Since my husband is a copywriter, we decided to set up a portfolio together and start going for interviews in some of London's hottest agencies. We wanted to get into Saint Luke's,

HHCL and we had also heard about this crazy little shop that had recently opened, called Mother ("What an interesting name for an agency", we thought at the time).

I called Mother where Yan Elliot and Luke Williamson finally had to meet us after receiving ten voicemails a day for two weeks. "I'm not going to give up," I said to Yan on my phone call number fifty, "so you better just agree to see us". We got to Mother and couldn't believe the place: an open space with just one huge table and, at the table, loads of people, including the Founding Partners who sat exactly at the same table. You could see in all their confident faces that they knew they were in the right place at the right time.

The guys had a look at our portfolio and loved it but they said we were too senior and they didn't need a senior team. So we asked them to sneak us in as a placement team and not tell anyone about our years of previous work in advertising, we would be just foreign students looking to gain experience. We wanted the job so badly that we wouldn't mind working for chicken feed. "They'll discover our talent," we said to ourselves, deep down, in a heroic Spanish internal voice over (including the echo). They thought we were crazy, but they didn't have anything to lose.

So we were in. "The Italian students," that's what we were called for a couple of weeks, until finally someone apart from Yan and Luke cared to understand that there was a country called Argentina, with which, by the way, England had been at war some years before. What followed was a fun story - now a bit of a myth inside Mother. After two weeks we cracked a Coke pitch by ourselves and got the account for the agency. So Robert Saville came and said: "Who the hell are you? You're not *students*, are you?"

We got a permanent job, and therefore, a first proper brief, maybe one of the most difficult briefs you can get: the agency's Christmas card. OMG, we thought, what a responsibility for a first production at Mother. Not only did we need to represent the agency and make them feel proud but everyone in the business would also be seeing this piece of work. We just couldn't mess around.

The budget, appalling: £5000 (nothing). Ok, we said, let's see, which means, let's start thinking, knowing that we will have to produce ourselves and/or pull in all the favors we can. We came up with what we thought was a nice idea: If Mother's motto was the truth and nothing but the truth about every brand, no matter how hard it comes, we had to depict the Christmas truth in a way that hadn't been seen before, using a kind of humor that represented Mother: irreverent, politically incorrect, but ultimately fun.

We created this Latino character called Chris Christmas Rodriguez, a guy who wanted to replace Santa (using the force if necessary) and bring some truth to the Christmas table. So with a series of spots, we would produce a viral campaign (remember we were in 1999, viral was a cool word then) that would go everywhere collecting votes for this man. We presented the scripts to the partners and they loved them. They also realized that this idea wouldn't fit in the budget available, nor did we have the time to produce it (this was October). We went back and said: We'll make it happen for £5000 and it will be on time.

We called a director in Buenos Aires who was just beginning his career (Luciano Podcaminsky) and he loved the idea; but he also knew it was a ridiculously tight budget. So we had to produce everything in a single day's shoot, with as few actors involved as possible. And it had to be made in Buenos Aires - London wouldn't work for that money.

Carlos and I already had flights back to Buenos Aires booked and paid for Christmas, so the only thing we did was a change the date. No additional cost for the production, great. Mark Waites, creative Director of Mother, wanted to come along but there wasn't enough money for the hotel, so we called my aunt and uncle and asked if they would accommodate us while we were shooting. We all ended up in a working class neighborhood in Buenos Aires, crowded into a small room.

But it happened. We did the shoot in a looooong one day (a twenty six hour shoot, so we had to take turns to sleep). And the outcome was fantastic. Mother loved the work and so did the people in the business. It was also an opportunity for Argentinian talent to shine in the UK market scene.

If you want to have a look at the work check this link:

http://www.youtube.com/watch?v=eokzuZK66v0

Today we are Founding Partners of Madre (the Latin American office of Mother), in Buenos Aires, the agency that we run since 2005.

Everything turned up great; but we had to take risks, like working for nothing and serving coffee in meetings after almost a decade of experience. By far, the best decision we've ever made.

Dorte Sengler-Ahrens
Chief Creative Officer
Jung von Matt/Fleet

Dörte started her career as an Junior Art Director in 1992 - three years later she became Creative Director at Jung von Matt.

She opened up her own company in 1999, called MARIA. But she missed the spirit of Jung von Matt and returned in 2000 to open up Jung von Matt/Spree in (funky funky) Berlin as CCO. Until then she worked in the international Jung von Matt Agency called JvM/9.

Until today she works as CCO of JvM/Fleet.

Dörte has worked for all important clients of the JvM Network, and is known for awardwinning work like "The WWF, the green file format" (a green and a golden pencil in One Show 2010), for DER SPIEGEL, BMW("Horses Ad"), Mercedes Benz, Zalando, and many many more.

Dörte is one of the most awarded German creatives.

She is member of the Art Directors Club Germany since 8/99, of D&AD, ADC NY, ADC Europe, Member of the Board of the Art Directors Club since 2002 (Responsible for Congresses,Seminars and Young Creatives)

In that function she invented and hosted the ADC BIC 08 (Germanys only Digital Congress for Brands and Communication)

Dörte was jury member in many international and national Awards like Eurobest (Jury President) 2001,Cannes Jury 2002, Euro ADC (7 times), ADC (every year), Clio 2007, ADC New York 2010, Asia Outdoor Awards, Clio 2011, LIAA 10, etc.

She loves to work, she loves her family, she loves to travel and meet people. If possible - everything at the same time.

My First Time
By Doerte Spengler-Ahrens

I remember clearly my first kiss, my first pet, (a budgie - he escaped the first night,) my first day at school, my first bicycle, my first party, my first ride in my first car, my first application, my first job,...I remember almost "my first everything".

Except my first ad.

It must have been so uninteresting, insignificant and simply unmemorable that it just slipped out of my memory. So I can only write about the first ad, I remember.

My first film was a funny concept with a famous German Comedian for a low fat cheese. My Executive Creative Director was so generous, to let "the girl" go to the shoot, too. It was so spontaneous, that I had no time to pack my things, and got a a toothbrush at the hotel desk. It was also my first night in a 4 Star Hotel. And my first stay in Hamburg. And my first visit to the famous Reeperbahn (red light district with restaurants and bars).

My first award was for my first ad in another agency called KNSK Hamburg for the "Lucky Strike" account, a cigarette brand. At that time the campaign was famous for their witty and humorous headlines, and I was very proud and I was literally lucky enough to work on that campaign, and to win a Gold in my first year on that account.

My first flop was another film. What happened? I relied on recommendations of some people I thought were more experienced than I - the film department of my agency, the boss of the film production. My gut feeling told me the whole time, that it was wrong. The actress was not good, the director was not inspired, the stylist was the girlfriend of somebody...

My first learning in execution: Paranoia pays. Never listen to "experts". Listen to your heart. Listen to your gut. Listen to yourself.

My first pitch success was at a very young age, we won a German newspaper- DIE WOCHE. My boss called me to come into his office and told me in a "between 4 eyes talk": Nice claim, dear. But it won't last until your pension..." I was 24.

My first grand prix was not an ad; but a product idea. And not only this, but a direct mail, a campaign, a nature initiative. All in one. It was a file format- a pdf you cannot print: the so called WWF. We just called it like that. It was for our client WWF. This product idea was the hardest work I ever did. One and a half years of endless tries to motivate companies (like adobe, apple, microsoft...) to help us, one and a half years to motivate people to work for us on a pro bono basis (it was social after all), to support us. One and a half years of struggling with investors, production companies, PR people, programmers, bosses, lawyers. At the end we did it ourselves. Without a core team of possessed people and my strong belief to succeed, we would never have made it.

My first lesson in realizing a big idea: "no" is not an option. Don't rely on anybody, except yourself and your team. And even if your boss, your board, your team, your attorney, your partners, AND your client lose confidence and courage- never give up. Call it killer instinct or obsession or devotion to ideas - only if you are frantic you will succeed.

My first thought when I was asked to contribute to this book was: what can I tell them? It is better to work together, then we can talk about something concrete.

My last words (our motto at JvM/Fleet) and last lesson:

I love what I do and I do what I love.

If you feel the same and want to do creative excellence, please contact me at Doerte.Spengler-Ahrens@jvm.de

Helayne Spivak
Director
VCU Brandcenter

Helayne Spivak, former Chief Creative Officer of Saatchi & Saatchi Wellness, joined the VCU Brandcenter on August 15, 2012 as its director. Helayne is leading the Brandcenter in its mission of helping the industry navigate change and fueling it with future leaders. She oversees financial and personnel management of the school, as well as fundraising and outreach to individuals and firms in the advertising industry and brand community.

Helayne began her award winning advertising career in NY as a copywriter at Ally & Gargano. After 10 years of gaining recognition for her creative work, Helayne went on to take larger and larger roles in the advertising community. Hal Riney hired her to head up the New York office of Hal Riney & Partners. From there, she went on to become Chief Creative Officer of Young & Rubicam NY as well being appointed one of the first women on their Board of Directors. She has since served as Chief Creative Officer of Ammirati Puris Lintas and Chief Creative Officer of JWT, NY. She has created campaigns for Sears (Come See the Softer Side of Sears), Burger King, UPS, Club Med, Kraft, Kodak, Barneys New York, and a U. S. President, to name just a few.

In 1997 Helayne formed her own company HRS Consulting where she worked with agencies such as Hill Holiday, McGarryBowen and EuroRSCG in New York and Chicago. After taking a 2-year break to buy and run a restaurant (long story available upon request), she returned to advertising in 2003 joining Energy BBDO in Chicago as Group Creative Director. In this role she ran Roche and the Bayer account including Aleve, OneADay Vitamins, Bayer Nutritional Science and Midol. Her Super Bowl spot for Aleve, featuring Leonard Nimoy, made USA Today's Top Ten Memorable spots for that year.

Helayne came back to NY in 2006 and was asked to join Saatchi & Saatchi Wellness to help them improve their creative product and move from an all DTC agency specializing in traditional broadcast advertising to a fully integrated, full channel communications company. In her 5 years as Chief Creative Officer, Saatchi & Saatchi Wellness have built their interactive capabilities from scratch, were named Agency Of The Year for 3 years running by MM&M Awards, and have already begun winning awards for their interactive work for a new MS drug, Transitions Lenses, and Durex. The newly formed Clio Healthcare Awards honored the agency's work for its "Silence Your Rooster" campaign with Best In Category and a Grand Clio.

Her extensive experience in the advertising business has given her the opportunity to work on herself or oversee work on an incredible range of clients in all industries: MCI, ATT, Sprint; UPS, FEDEX, USPS; American Express, MasterCard, Bayer, Bristol Myers, Ciba-Geigy, American Home Products, Reebok, General Motors, Fuji, Kodak, MONY, Johnson & Johnson, Kraft, Colgate, Philip Morris, Dr. Pepper, Cadbury Schweppes, Club Med, Burger King, Four Seasons Hotels, Andrew Jergens Company, Shiseido, Bill Blass, Vanity Fair Magazine and The New Yorker.

Over the course of the years Helayne has been recognized by The Wall Street Journal's Leaders Campaign, was honored with The Matrix Award for Women in Communications, appeared on the cover of Working Woman Magazine for which she wrote the cover article, was named one of the top 50 Women In Business by Business Week magazine (1992), served as a judge on the television panel at the Cannes Advertising Festival, was a member of the board of directors of The One Club, and has received many individual awards for her work from the Clio Awards (including best writer), The One Club, Cannes, The Andy's, and the Effie's.

My First Time(s)
By Helayne Spivak

I was a 22-year-old kid right in the middle of a 6-week portfolio course at
The School of Visual Arts. I did my entire portfolio in record time, over
one weekend, around my 3rd week of class because my teacher, Tom
Messner, said there was a Junior position open over at his agency Carl
Ally Inc. He said could get me an interview on Monday if I could get my
book together.

So I did a book that consisted of 10 "clever" one-off ads, one sort-of-a-
campaign and no TV (drew the ads myself on tracing paper, did my own
lettering, did my own scrap pasting layouts and stapled the results to pieces
of white drawing paper and slipped the whole thing into acetate sleeves
inside a leather portfolio) This was pre-Photoshop. Pre-1984 Macintosh.
But well after Magic Markers.

I showed my book to Amil Gargano and Jim Durfee on Monday, got the
offer on Tuesday, accepted on Wednesday. I had my first job.

My first ad was to introduce Pan Am's new Wide-bodied Planes: the 747
and the 747SP. I barely could find my way to where the coffee machine
was but I sat down with a very senior art director who took pity on me and
we started throwing out lines. Everything I said started out…"Maybe this
sounds stupid but"….or "I know this sounds ridiculous but"…And he,
because he was wonderful and generous, would encourage me until I said
"hey, how about YOU'LL LOVE US FOR OUR BODIES". He loved it.
(Thank you, Howard Benson). My supervisor Tom Messner loved it. I
had gotten my very first full page NY Times ad approved. Then the Pan
Am client saw it and said it was too "sexy". So, later that day, I had also
gotten my very first ad rejection.

A few weeks later, I was fortunate enough to get my very first radio
campaign because the woman who had been assigned to it didn't want to

lower herself to do something as mundane as a radio campaign and the due date was quickly approaching. So Tom gave me the assignment with the kind of detailed direction that I always appreciated: "Here. Go do it. "

So the producer and I did the casting, directed the recordings, I wrote the personal stories for the actors - about what it was like going back with Pan Am to discover the second heritage every American had. For that assignment that no one else wanted to touch, I won my first Clio for a national Radio Campaign.

God, I loved this business.

This was where a woman could work alongside a man and because a finished ad is pretty gender neutral, it could have been done by a man or a woman - who cares as long as the work was great? None of that sexist, chauvinistic crap going on in this industry.

Next, I got a terrific assignment. A series of funny, sarcastic, competitive radio spots for MCI while they were in the process of taking down AT&T (it was so long ago, AT&T still had the ampersand & a building on Park Avenue).

So I wrote a series of humorous radio plays pointing out the absurdity of spending more than you had to on Long Distance. One was about calling after 11 PM, entitled "Reach Out And Wake Someone". Another was about AT&T Reaching Out For Your Wallet. You get the idea. They got a lot of attention. And another award.

I was standing in the hall at the agency talking to a male art director friend of mine when my supervisor, Tom Messner, came by with the MCI client. This was the client that had approved the radio campaign for which I had just won the award. We had never met. Tom said to the MCI client, "hey, how would you like to meet the great mind behind your new radio campaign?" And the guy reached right over me to the man I was standing with and he shook his hand and said, "Hey, man. You're doing a great job."

I did a little wave and said, "I think *I'm* your man", and we all did a little embarrassed laugh. (Well, I wouldn't say the art director was really embarrassed. He was too busy blowing his coffee out through his nose).

That was the first time I realized that gender blindness is in the eyes of the beholder. That was my first inkling of gender bias, but not the last. However, judging from my career, I never let a little under-estimation get in the way of succeeding. But let's look around us. What percentage of high-level creative directors are women? How many are leaders of major corporations? How many are at the forefront of the emerging start-up technology companies? (And if the number is as low as I believe it is, take look at who's getting the lion's share of the VC funding).

Women will always have to fight a little harder to make their contributions to the world. Unless, of course, we wake up tomorrow and start to judge people by their actions and talent and decency and not their gender or race or religious beliefs. Now THAT would be a first.

Emer Stamp
Joint Executive Creative Director, Adam&Eve DDB

Over the last 12 years Emer and her long-suffering partner Ben, have worked their way through some of London's top creative agencies, including Leagas Delaney, MCBD, DDBLondon and Adam&Eve. By a strange twist of fate she is now Joint Executive Creative Director of the recently merged Adam&EveDDB with, yes, you guessed it...

My First Time
By Emer Stamp

"Who the fuck are *you*?"

Those were Tim Delaney's first words to us. And he was right to ask. Who the fuck *were* we?

Pure luck had landed us a job at Leagas Delaney. We had sent our portfolio in to a senior creative with a note attached, asking him if he would consider putting us forward for a job. He was on paternity leave, so our book and note were passed on to another team.

I now know that if Mr. Paternity Leave had seen it we would never have even got as far as an interview. But, as I said, luck was with us. The other team liked our book. We had a chat, then they had a chat with Tim and we got the job. Our first job together as 'Ben & Emer'.

It was the summer of 2000, it was baking hot, and we were working in a building without air conditioning. I remember that every few minutes I had to wipe the sweat off my palms so that my pen wouldn't slip out of my hands. And oh how I needed that pen.

My contract stated that I was an Art Director, but what miniscule Art Directional skills I had at that point where rarely called upon. Ben and I were first and foremost, writers. Frantic writers, frantic, shit-scared writers, with over-heating palms.

I am not sure if you know much about the Myth of Leagas Delaney, but it was all true. There was no working week, there was just working. We got a day off on Saturdays because that was the day Tim went to watch the football.

It was reputed that he had once said to a team, "If you don't come in on Christmas Day then don't bother coming in on Boxing Day".

He was, and still is, a brilliant writer. I would go as far to say, in the UK at least, he is the Godfather of the headline. And, as you can imagine, it's no easy task trying to impress a man who could wipe the literary floor with you with one flourish of his Mont Blanc fountain pen.

I seem to recall the first brief we were ever given was for a quarter page announcing the start of the Harrods' sale. It was made clear from the outset that all that was required was, 'simply a headline'. Simply my arse. No one 'simply' got a headline through Tim.

We naively bashed out what we thought were some right witty corkers. I remember being particularly pleased with one that talked of early birds and worms. We gathered up our offerings, all neatly marker-penned onto individual sheets of A4, and made our way to his small, windowless, office (never judge power on office size or window footage).

We sat down and passed over our handful of lines. One minute later we were back in our office starting over again.

We learnt fast that you never presented Tim with a 'handful' of lines. You always presented him with at least an inch – and by that I mean the thickness of the paper when you held them all together. And you didn't need to write them up all neatly. He didn't care how they came. As long as they came. So we tore reams of A4 in half, placed them in a huge pile in the center of our desk, then wrote, scribbled and scrawled on them until we felt we had exhausted every possible permutation of words pertinent to the brief.

Then we went back to the small, windowless office and crossed everything bendy on our bodies. If you were lucky, Tim would make three piles: Yes, No and Maybe. If you were unlucky there was just one pile and it was back to the drawing board. And the Yes's were never a Yes until you had gone away and sweated the Maybe's – just in case there was some missed genius in them.

Painful as it was, I believe it was the best training we could have had. We learnt how to write and we learnt that even when you think there is nothing left in the pot it's always worth one more look.

Tim also taught us that headline writing doesn't just crack a print or poster brief. It can crack almost any brief. A great headline is a clever thought, and a clever thought is at the heart of everything we do.

We spent almost three years at Leagas Delaney before being headhunted by another agency. I remember our new Creative Director commenting on a particular piece in our portfolio, "Oh, you're the guys that wrote this, I love this line. Great piece of writing".

And just like that, someone knew who the fuck we were.

Nancy Vonk
Co-founder of Swim

Nancy Vonk was Co-Chief Creative Officer of Ogilvy Toronto before founding a creative leadership training lab, Swim, with long-time partner Janet Kestin in 2011.

They have won many top industry awards including Cannes Lions, One Show Pencils and Clios. They are the creative directors of Dove "Evolution", winner of two Grand Prix at Cannes, and "Diamond Shreddies, winner of a Grand Clio.

Nancy has judged many of the world's top advertising awards shows including Cannes, Clios, One Show and D&AD. In '08 she was the first female chair in the history of the Art Director's Club of New York.

Nancy and Janet's honors include being named to Creativity magazine's Top 50 creative people of '08, advertising Women of the Year at the WIN Awards in LA and the AWNY Awards in NY in '07, and induction into Canada's Marketing Hall of Legends in '11.

They have a widely read advice column, "Ask Jancy" on ad site ihaveanidea.org. They penned a critically acclaimed Adweek book, "Pick Me", in 2005. It has become a staple in advertising schools from Texas to Turkey. They are currently writing a business book for HarperCollins.

Nancy is a mentor and frequent lecturer at ad schools including the renowned VCU Brandcenter. She has been on the board of the One Club since '09.

My First Time
By Nancy Vonk

Our family lore has it that before I could talk, I would often stand in front of the bathroom mirror holding a bottle of dish liquid and babble in tones recognizable from the TV commercials of the day. I was holding something VERY SPECIAL up to that glass. My big fake smile, wide eyes and animated body language made that clear. So technically, I cranked out my first ad around age 2.

I became that kid who was drawing constantly, always the best artist in class. By 7ish I vividly remember drawing a sort of storyboard for an Ivory soap commercial. I was inspired by the tiny silver bubbles that radiated from the bar when I held it under a blast of water in the tub. I wanted everyone to know how amazing this was, and television was the obvious place to reach my target of everyone. (No savant, strategic thinking wouldn't show up until a couple of decades later.)

Now, you would think a career in advertising or some other creative field might naturally unfold with this kind of foreshadowing. But I was well into my university years before I stopped balking at channeling my creative talents into a living. I thought that would wreck everything. Art was supposed to be fun, not a job. It eventually dawned on me that using what you're reasonably good at is how it works. I had numerous summer jobs to underscore my incompetence at anything related to math or physical labor.

I had report cards filled with evidence I should really narrow things down to either art or writing. One English prof strongly advised against a job in journalism when I showed interest. (She was a bitter, former journalist.) I stumbled into "graphic communications" at the University of Delaware after attending a dynamic presentation about the program given by the young head of the department, Ray Nichols. As I considered a major in art history, art education, fine arts and photography, suddenly advertising jumped out. "That looks like fun" is about as deep and complex as the thought process went as I chose my path.

The program was very intense; our class of 60 dropped to 12 by the time I graduated. I left school with a good portfolio and a lot of experience with all-nighters and high stress. I was first in my major, and felt pretty well prepared for the "real world", but in short order I was thrown by how protracted the job search proved to be. After about 14 interviews in the D.C. area I was feeling desperate. (Genius reason to look there? Home of my two best friends.) I was on the all-Cheerios, all-the-time diet and was willing to work for a printing house with an opening for a "paste-up" artist at this point. I had the first big break of my career: the kindly owner said he'd be happy to hire me, but advised I should keep looking for what I went to school to accomplish. The very next interview was in posh Georgetown, at a tiny shop of maybe 17 people. Bingo. I was a junior art director.

I didn't have that first job people like Sally Hogshead and Ted Royer can look back on loaded with global awards, stellar accounts and high profile creative leaders. While little Sal and Ted were at the pode accepting hardware, I was designing menus and hotel brochures. I was doing mechanicals, changing the chemicals in the dark room, and making some minor contribution to the creative director's ads on occasion. I was so excited to see "my" ad in Time magazine (a redesign of an existing ad done by someone else). To think my parents would add that very issue to their giant stack of Time's in the basement closet---amazing.

Designing a program for a Lena Horne concert was another thrill. (Photo provided, no shoot or actual contact with the diva.) We often worked with talented photographers and illustrators; the awards I recall were craft awards for their work. I got to shoot with Bret Littlehales and was so impressed he shot for National Geographic, as his father had before him.

Looking back, I was in exactly the right place for me. It wasn't my first, second or 13th choice. At this tiny shop I got a view to the way the whole

224

agency worked. I got to make lots of mistakes without penalty. I learned about teamwork. I learned from wonderful people including an absolute wild woman, Sam Macuga, the creative director. I emulated her bold style and fearlessness (though I had to fake that for a good while). Gender was a non-event, to watch her in action. It didn't occur to me for a very long time that some women have a hard go based on gender.

I went up the ladder slowly, but surely. In my first job I had no ambition but to not be fired. I was painfully insecure and part of my successful journey was thanks to others believing in me. I was bossy as all get-out since birth, but it wasn't on my to-do list to lead and in fact I had to be pushed to take bigger and bigger titles over the years.

I think everything happens for a reason, and timing is everything. Things worked out, in spite of my first ad being so inconsequential, I can't remember it. (Unless you count the age-7 Ivory commercial, which to be fair, wasn't produced.)

Your first job doesn't have to be at Crispin or R/GA or Droga5. You will learn valuable lessons anywhere. If you don't shoot to the ad stratosphere in record time, or any time soon, fret not. By all means, knock on the doors where you'd kill to work. But when those very few dream openings go to others, believe me, there is reason to go on living.

Susan Westre
Executive Creative Director
Ogilvy

"As a youngster, my passions were to paint and travel. When I discovered that advertising would pay me to travel the world, my career choice was made."

At Ogilvy and Mather, Susan is the Worldwide Creative Director on the IBM account. Her work extends from the original ebusiness campaign to the Smarter Planet campaign running today. In 2011, the story of an IBM Supercomputer competing against 2 humans in the American Game show *Jeopardy!* won both Gold and Silver Lions.

During her tenure on the account, IBM's brand ranking has gone from 287 to the second most valuable brand in the world. Susan finds herself lucky to be working on a brand that is actually trying to make the world a better place.

Susan has enjoyed focusing on clients who need big, global ideas at Ogilvy. Before Ogilvy, Susan worked at BBDO in Los Angeles (where she hated the traffic) and CLM/BBDO in Paris (where she loved the food).

Her work for IBM, Apple, SAP, Pepsi and Kodak has been awarded at Cannes, The One Show, The Webby's, The Clios, The Effies, The Art Director's Club, The London International Festival, D&AD, and Communication Arts. During her career, she was named an Adweek National Creative All-Star for Art Direction, received a "Best Campaign of the Year" award from both AdAge and AdWeek and two Grand Effies; one for IBM and one for Apple.

Susan is married with two wonderful daughters, and divides her time between the Paris and New York offices.

My First Time
By Susan Westre

This is a story about 3 firsts: my first job, my first TV commercial, and my big break in advertising which lead to my first important package of commercials.

Notice that my big break comes third in this story - it was 6 years after my first job.

As a young art student at the University of Wisconsin, Madison, I aspired to be a painter. But as the time to being a starving artist drew near, a friend told me about "advertising" and suggested that with my artistic ability, I could be an art director.

Mind you, I had never heard of such a job before, but I liked the sound of it.

With my University degree and not much else, I landed my first job as a paste-up artist and part-time receptionist in a tiny ad agency in Milwaukee Wisconsin. I took night classes, moved on to a better job at a wonderful, young agency called Frankenberry, Laughlin and Constable, and after 3 years in the business, landed in Los Angeles. My incredibly humble beginning in advertising taught me about production, deadlines, and the craft of making an ad look beautiful.

Los Angeles was not as hospitable as I hoped, but brought me in contact with some wonderful and quirky people. With my meager book, I couldn't even get an interview at Chiat/Day, but I landed an art director job at an agency that was half Mormon, half Jewish, and had one very brilliant young copywriter. His name was Chris Wall, and he had come off of the copy desk of The May Company. At the time, he seemed more interested in playing basketball and writing puns than making world-class advertising. But the puns eventually stopped, and we formed a creative partnership that lasted over 20 years and four agencies.

Our first TV commercial was for Del Mar Mini-Blinds. The concept – redecorate a real prison cell in Alcatraz. The commercial was a fake-out: you thought you were looking at a normal room, only to have the camera pull out to reveal that it was a prison cell. "Using only a little paint and some imagination, you can improve any room". We had a budget of $80,000, which meant we could spent a week prepping and shooting in San Francisco, and compose original music.

During the prep week, when the cell (hospital ward cell with window) was being repainted and decorated in lovely colors, tourists would wander by, making comments like "that was Al Capone's cell – they are just renovating it."

We had to do a night shoot. Alcatraz at night is one of the creepiest places I've ever been. There are strange noises and groans, and to a person, we went to the chemical toilet on the other end of the cell-block in twos all night long. If we were doing that commercial today, the possibilities for "behind the scenes" and design tutorials would be endless. I learned back then that if you make a hero out of the product, and surround it with an interesting story, it is not hard to get the client to buy an interesting idea.

My big break came in Los Angeles when a colleague went to BBDO "Slightly Further West" as traffic manager, and told Steve Hayden that he should meet Chris and me. Steve Hayden was the man who had authored most of Apple's acclaimed print advertising, and had written the ground-breaking "1984" commercial at Chiat/Day the year before. We put together a portfolio of our work plus some ideas that had never been produced.

Our meeting with Steve went fine, (both Chris and I remember him staring at us without blinking much) but we didn't think we stood a chance. So after meeting Steve, we put together a reminder of who we were: a little program called "HeadHunter" that was a digital rolodex in HyperCard, where you could catalogue creative talent – it was filled with our names and silly pictures. Steve was so amused by Headhunter that he hired us -- plus we were cheap and ready to do anything to work on the Apple computer account.

To work on Apple TV, we had to compete with the creative department of BBDO New York, which was filled with heavy-hitters. But unlike Chris and me, they didn't use the product. We lived and breathed Macintosh, and it came through in our work. The first Apple campaign we sold was 6 spots, which lead to 6 weeks of shooting with the directing legend, Joe Pytka. It was an education by fire. When Joe met us, he greeted us with "who the fuck are you?"

This was the first package of spots we had ever produced. Up until then, it was one spot at a time. The campaign demonstrated how Macintosh could change the way people lived, worked or expressed themselves. I spent sleepless nights designing the graphics on the Macintosh screens for these commercials and then struggled to find people who could produce them. At the time, there were about 10 illustrators in the country who could actually make beautiful illustrations on the computer. This was pre-Windows and the graphical user interface was still unique to Apple. All of the computer screens had to be shot "live". In order to do that, we needed a specialist on the set who synched up the monitor to work with the camera's film speed - a skillset that was extremely hard to find.

Each spot in the pool had some major drama during the production. Our first commercial was about a new teacher and her classroom of 8-year-olds. About two hours into the shoot, the cell phone of the computer specialist rang during a take. Cell phones were forbidden on the set. Joe's key grip, a former Hell's Angel named Tommy, decided to teach this computer nerd a lesson, and he verbally attacked him in a very Hell's Angel sort of way. At which point the computer specialist started pulling out all the cords on his equipment saying, "there are two or three great directors in this city. But there is only *one* of me."

231

The shoot came to a dead halt as he walked off the set. Four hours later, after Joe talked him back into it, he returned to the set. We managed to shoot the spot, where the teacher uses computer wizardry to impress the class by replacing Mona Lisa's face with the face of one of the students. It was quite charming, and went on to win a Gold Lion at Cannes that year, but we didn't even know what Cannes was back then.

What did I learn from this first pool of spots? Know the product better than your competition. It means you will come up with better stories. Anticipate the director. Be prepared. Never assume anything. Be willing to make changes to your idea, script, or cast if something isn't turning out great, and make sure the client understands why you are making the changes. And work with the best talent you can find, even if they are difficult. A short period of discomfort during production is quickly forgotten when the result is great work that can live on for years.

About the Author

Phil Growick is the Managing Director of the Howard-Sloan-Koller Group in New York City, the retained executive search firm specializing in top talent in all forms of advertising and media.

His friendships with some of the world's most influential advertising creatives led to the creation of the *My First Time* series.

The first in the series, was *My First Time*, with 43 top ECDs and CCOs from all over the world.

Future editions will include:

My First Time, Jr.

My First Time 2

Many more are planned.

Phil's first Sherlock Holmes novel, *The Secret Journal of Dr. Watson*, was published this past May. A sequel is in the works. At that time, all the questions left unanswered, will be.

When not working with and enjoying his advertising friends, he dotes on his wife, his sons, his daughter-in-law and all animals. Except werewolves.

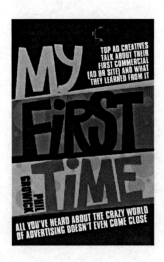

Lightning Source UK Ltd.
Milton Keynes UK
UKOW040931101012

200347UK00006B/42/P